MODERN PROCESS THOUGHT

A Brief Ideological History

James R. Gray
Department of Philosophy
Howard University

UNIVERSITY
PRESS OF
AMERICA

BD
372
.G7
1982

Library of Congress Catalog Card Number: **81-43672**

DEDICATED TO Maria Flora Gray and
Ellen A. Wheeler

ACKNOWLEDGMENTS

I would like to express my appreciation to Professor D.W.D. Shaw of St. Andrew's University, Scotland, for his many useful suggestions about the text; and the faculty and staff of New College, Edinburgh, where much of the research was completed. Dr. William A. Banner of Howard University was also kind enough to review the manuscript, and I am grateful for his advice. Dr. Max Wilson, Chairman of the Department of Philosophy at Howard University, has made every effort to assist me with the publication of this book. Without this support it would not have been possible. Special thanks is owed to Mr. Perry J. Putnam, whose help and support was a part of every stage of the preparations. Finally I would like to thank the University Press of America and its staff for making this publication possible. Weaknesses in the text are my sole responsibility, as they could not reflect the excellent help that I have received.

TABLE OF CONTENTS

PREFACE

I began this book as a reference for persons interested in the history of Process Thought. In its present form the work has become somewhat more. It is also a study of some of the ways that biology and physics shaped a significant part of twentieth century philosophy. Therefore, it may serve as a resource for any student of contemporary philosophy, and the history of ideas.

The understanding of the term absolute appears as a theme which helps to demonstrate the connections between the various influences on the development of Process. In spite of my repeated reference to this theme, I do not believe that it has been given too much emphasis.

The first nine Chapters concentrate more on the influences that the scientific community has had on Process. Chapters Ten through Seventeen are concerned with the more philosophical influences, in particular the epistemological ones. The consideration of Process from a theological perspective fills the last several Chapters. These topics can be considered independently of one another; but their particular interrelatedness, within Process, can best be understood when they are considered in the order presented.

INTRODUCTION

This book is designed to introduce Process philosophy through a study of the history of its development. In order to do this, one must begin with certain philosophical and scientific influences of the late nineteenth century. From that time until the present Process thought developed and matured in the minds of men such as Henri Bergson, Samuel Alexander, Teilhard de Chardin, Alfred North Whitehead, Charles Hartshorne, and Norman Pittenger.

The term 'Process' is actually used in two different ways. First, 'Process' is a position which contends that the entire universe, including God, is in a constant state of change. Second, 'process' is used to describe the particular kind of change. According to this view, process is universal activity understood as a continuity of antecedences and consequences brought about by an interrelation between 'true' diversity and true 'unity'.

For those who are somewhat familiar with Process, or for those who know nothing about it, it can best be associated with the development of theories of 'relativity'. In particular the topic of relationships dominates the works of those authors who are called Process philosophers.

In Process terms relativity itself is a relationship between a principle of absoluteness and a principle of relatedness. Process thinkers say that the universe is 'di-polar'. That it is composed of complementary aspects of absoluteness and relatedness.

This book begins with an analysis of the fact that a confrontation between scientific mechanism and vitalism, in the late nineteenth and early twentieth centuries, contributed to the development of what is today called "Process Philosophy". During this same period, in which new sciences arose and old sciences were transformed, men, who were sensative to metaphysical questions, became aware of a pressing demand to establish tests for classical cosmologies against the rapid advances made in scientific research. One of the first dilemmas to emerge from these efforts was that, from a metaphysical viewpoint, the sciences were producing conflicting data in support of both absolute mechanism and also ultimate pluralism (the one and the many; absoluteness and relativity.)

However, the development of Process thought cannot be understood only as a response to modern science. Its development was aided because Process thinkers had a solid grounding in philosophical tradition.

"Dipolarity" is both a philosophical and also a scientific position. From a philosophical viewpoint of dipolarity an absolute pole always appears in company with a relative pole. Together these poles function in realizing the universal principle of process, which may be thought of as an 'abstract' principle. From a scientific viewpoint, taken separately each pole has a 'concrete' content. To be fully understood the poles must be considered in both their abstract and concrete aspects.

For modern thinkers it is perhaps the absolute pole which is most difficult to comprehend. Therefore, let us consider how the term 'absolute' is used by Process. Kant, for example, observed that the term absolute is applied in two senses. First in the narrow sense it means that "something is true of a thing in itself."[1] In terms of this usage one might say that the relative pole is absolutely relative, or that the principle of process is absolutely a process.

Process thought would agree with the Kantian suggestion that such a usage of the term absolute is ambiguous. It, with Kant, would favor a wider use of the term, which is described by Kant as implying that something is the same "in every relation possible." According to this wider usage something referred to as absolute must have an inner necessity, which remains the same in all possible relations. In this sense the relative pole cannot be absolute. The entities which make up its content vary from instant to instant. On the other hand, the absolute pole does have an inner necessity by which it is, abstractly considered, always the same.

Having agreed that the term absolute should be used in the wider sense, the ambiguous nature of the term is not resolved. When the term absolute is applied in the widest possible sense one may assume that (1) it refers to the total content of the universe as a unified Given, or (2) that it refers to an attribute of some ultimate, universal principle. The former empasizes the fact that the absolute has all reality as its concrete content, while the latter suggests that absoluteness is a characteristic of an abstract principle, which in turn directs all reality. The former suggests that the absolute 'is' the unity of all reality; the latter suggests that an absolute principle 'functions' to unify all reality.

The point to be observed is that Process thought accepts neither of these interpretations of the wider meaning of the term absolute. While it does say that the absolute pole has a concrete content, the acceptance of the relative pole means that this cannot be all of reality. Likewise, while Process does say that absoluteness applies to an abstract principle, this principle does not function apart from the relative pole, and thus it does not direct all reality.

What Process does suggest is that both of the above interpretations of the term absolute are significant only when taken together and in the context of a dipolar universe. This view leads to a new understanding of the term 'absolute', but it does not lack connections with traditional meanings. The understanding is that of a 'role'; implying that the absolute pole has a definite character of its own and also plays a part in the cosmic drama.

How Process reached the conclusion of the complementary nature of an absolute pole and a relative pole is one of the topics of this book. We must begin

with a consideration of how the history of certain scientific developments, during the end of the last century
and the beginning of our present century, influenced
the formulation of new understandings of the terms
absolute and relative.

At the beginning of our period of study, the
guiding principle of most scientific investigations
was a conviction that the cosmos was ultimately mechanistic. Mechanism is a position which holds that a
single absolute principle of order underlies reality.

Given the presupposition of an absolute order,
the test for scientific validity was the discovery of
how various aspects of the phenomenal world exemplified
this order. One must not believe that many scientific
laws implied an ultimate pluralism. Many laws could
share the attribute of absoluteness, because they
could be interpreted as consistent formulations of the
single absolute law of cosmic order.

Mechanism was popular because it worked. With
the help of Newtonian physics and metaphysics, the
sciences reached new heights of achievement. Because
mechanism then dominated science and greatly influenced metaphysics, and because the assumption of
absolute physical laws was a key to their procedures,
any position, such as Process, which rejects pure
mechanism, must confront the question of absolute
order.

To even suggest that physical laws are not
absolute is to suggest that the universe is chaotic --
the position of some existentialists. Nevertheless,
Process felt it necessary to call mechanism into
question. The issue which science raised for Process
metaphysics is whether or not scientific data support
the conclusion that philosophy must always choose
between absolute pyhsical order or total chaos.

We will begin with discussing mechanism, and see
how it could be rejected. The choice to reject
mechanism was not made first by Process thinkers.

German idealisms, which dominated philosophy near the early part of our period of study, illustrate, unlike mechanism, an understanding of the absolute as that which contained all reality. In the context of a conflict between these two positions, Process philosophy developed.

No sooner had scientific mechanism matured than philosophical idealism challenged it. The chief difference between the two systems is summarized by saying that mechanism was materialistic, while idealism was spiritualistic. Spiritualism centered many of its formulations around explanations for the existence of human self-consciousness, which it argued could not be explained in terms of absolute physical laws. The unity of a universe containing consciousness had to be of a spiritual order. The source of unity was not a physical principle, but a supreme 'Subject'.

As only an absolute Subject -- God -- could account for a universe containing consciousness, the absolute Subject can also be thought of as the ground of consciousness. Spiritualism also suggests that material laws cannot provide ultimately valid knowledge.

With reference to whether absoluteness should be attributed to a concrete Subject or an abstract physical principle, idealism and mechanism hold opposite positions. However, Process thought rejected both on the grounds that they lead to determinism. In a very important sense Process developed as a response to, and an alternative for, both idealism and mechanism.

Of course, what has just been said requires fuller development. However, it is important to note that the question of absoluteness and unity related and divided many sciences and philosophies in the late nineteenth and early twentieth centuries. In attempting to understand these divisions, Process thinkers arrived at dipolarity as the essential principle of relatedness in the universe.

Close on the heels of metaphysics are the philosophical discussions concerning the nature of human
knowledge -- including self-knowledge. Epistemology,
as this branch of philosophy is called, is an important topic in the history of Process thought.

For example, as we have said mechanism and idealism demonstrate opposite metaphysical positions.
Epistemologically, however, idealism and mechanism are
rather similar, as well as different. They are similar
in the fact that for both the content of knowledge is
determined. For mechanism knowledge is merely knowing the absolute physical laws; and for idealism
knowledge is knowing an absolute Subject. They differ
as to whether knowledge is acquired through experience
or introspection.

Mechanism insists that knowledge comes from
experience -- but it is experience of absolute laws.
Idealism holds that knowledge is chiefly innate. In
the mid-nineteenth century certain forms of 'realism'
developed as the epistemological alternative to both
positions.

Important to Process thought is that certain
philosophers attempted to develop an anti-mechanistic
realism. These were epistemologies that combined the
principles of realism with scientific pluralism. They
rejected both absolute mechanism and Absolute Subject.
Anti-mechanistic scientific realism contributed to the
development of Process.

On the one hand, this book surveys the general
development of Process thought. However, the most
fully developed and influential Process cosmology is
that of Alfred North Whitehead. Because of this, our
book gives his works special attention. We will
discover that, after Whitehead, the majority of pro-
minent Process thinkers are either his students, or
otherwise greatly influenced by the "Whiteheadian
School".

The latter stages of Process find it being

developed into a theology. In a history of the development of Process thought, one must certainly include the theological developments that occurred. Whitehead laid the groundwork for such a development. Although he was clearly a philosopher rather than a theologian.

One of the reasons for Whitehead's influence is his consistency in developing the implications of the concept of process throughout his cosmology. In the case of most other writers, who are sympathetic to the concept of process, not all of their works are dominated by the concept in the sense that Whitehead's are. This means that in the case of certain writers we will tend to consider only the portions of their works which do, in our opinion, reflect the idea of the concept of process. In other words, we will point to the respects in which they are Process thinkers. Realizing that one could make a good case for the fact that their works contain other elements as well. We have, of course, attempted not to misrepresent the overall tone of a writer's position by searching for the Process aspects of his thinking.

1 Kant's CRITIQUE OF PURE REASON. trans., Norman
    Kemp Smith. (London: Macmillan, 1929). pp. 316-
    318.

CHAPTER I

MECHANISM

The term 'mechanism' as applied here refers to the position, characteristic of the physical sciences in the late nineteenth century, that all occurrences in the phenomenal world follow fixed material laws, which reflect an absolute principle of cosmic order. The function of this principle is to predetermine all events causally. Moreover, the term mechanistic may be used in a wider sense to describe many of the scientific, philosophical and metaphysical positions at the end of the nineteenth century. Our first purpose is this Chapter is to illustrate mechanism by showing how widespread was the scientific conviction that reality is absolutely ordered. Second we will show that mechanism suggests a particular understanding of the term absolute, and we will see how this relates to Spiritualism's understanding of the term.

As applied toward the end of the nineteenth century, the term mechanistic refers to the position, generally adopted by the physical sciences, especially physics itself, which maintains that the laws governing the material world are applicable, without exception, to all reality. As James Ward said "...mechanical explanation has therefore long been accepted as the ne plus ultra of what a scientific explanation can be."1

From the scientific viewpoint the phrase "without exception" was used with real confidence only after the middle of the nineteenth century. And it was this part of the mechanistic explanation which became a key issue for philosophy -- and for the new science of Biology. Biology seemed to indicate an ultimate plurality of life forms.

Indeed the reason for many of the strong reactions against mechanism during this period was the boldness with which physical science applied it to the phenomenon of life. There had been earlier attempts

1

to present a purely mechanistic interpretation of life. Descartes, in his works DE HOMINE and DE FORMATIONS FOETUS, is the most outstanding example. However, wide acceptance of such a view, even among scientists, did not take place until the mid-nineteenth century.

William McDougall, in his book BODY AND MIND, 1911, suggests that three key factors in the scientific world accounted generally for this wider acceptance of mechanism. These three factors were: (1) the mechanistic account of evolution suggested by Darwin's principle of adaptation through natural selection; (2). the discovery in physiology that the brain is a vast and complex system of reflex nerve paths; (3). the establishment of the law of the conservation of energy.2 These points require some development.

Charles Darwin radically changed the scientific approach to life. His two greatest contributions were the establishment of evolution as an incontestable fact; and the identification of natural selection as a major element in adaptation.

Essentially Darwin viewed natural selection as a factor in the process of elimination of those individuals that did not show the characteristics which happened to be useful for the survival of their species of organism. However, to grasp the mechanistic nature of natural selection one must see it in terms of Darwin's theory of 'descent', which Hans Driesch describes as; "The theory of descent is the hypothetic statement that the organisms are really allied by blood among each other, in spite of their diversities."3

The chief characteristics of each species are supposedly passed materially between generations by some undetermined process of heredity, i.e. some abstract physical principle. Slection is, so to speak, the elimination by chance of any defective products of this heredity.

To say that natural selection totally explained

2

adaptation was impossible. Adaptation thus explained
continues to have the appearance of purposefulness,
which eliminates its purely mechanistic explanation.
In the hands of the Neo-Darwinians, however, natural
selection was an even closer ally for physical
mechanism. The fluctuating variations in organisms
were explained as accidental differences in the arrangements of particles of matter in the blood, and nothing
more.4

The theory of natural selection as the explanation for adaptation is biology's contribution to the
popularity of the mechanistic theory. The second
contribution, that of psycho-physical parallelism, was
made by the emerging science of physiology. Henri
Bergson gives a very concise definition of parallelism.
He says that parallelism assumes that physiological
brain states and psychical mental states are always
parallel.5

Physiology's discovery of the nervous system and
its biochemical functioning was the primary source for
the concept of parallelism. Based on these discoveries
the assumption was made that all mental processes
could be explained by the purely mechanistic laws of
brain chemistry. We will return to the subject of
parallelism when we consider certain objections to it.

The third, and in the minds of many the most conclusive, argument for a mechanistic theory was the
establishment of the law of the conservation of energy,
the first law of thermodynamics, and the theory of
entropy, the second law of thermodynamics. This is a
contribution made by physics to the mechanistic theory.

Simply stated, the first law of thermodynamics
is that energy can be neither created nor destroyed.
The best way to show why this would suggest mechanism
is through an example, such as the following one used
by Haldane: "Any 'guidance' of living organisms by the
vital principle would imply a creation or destruction
of energy; and this would be the case even if the
energy created in the living substance were again

destroyed before it could escape to the outside, and so become measurable."6

In other words, anything which alters the physical laws could do so only by the creation or destruction of energy, which according to thermodynamics is impossible. In all cases, even in the case of life, the mechanistic laws apply without exception. This also means that no truly unique factor can be introduced into the universe; rather our understanding of the laws of nature can only be expanded or refined.

The second law of thermodynamics is the law of entropy. Ward defines entropy as, "The steady downward trend, the katabolic, leveling tendencies attributed to unchecked mechanism..."7 The theory of entropy stems in part from the introduction of potential energy to accompany the then established theory of kinetic energy. With the introduction of the concept of potential energy, activity became understood as the conversion of potential into kinetic energy. According to the theory of entropy the potential energy in the universe will eventually be depleted and all activity will cease.

The suggestion of the possibility of an entropic state arose from the observation that areas having various temperatures (differing potentials) demonstrated a tendency to establish a unified temperature. Once this occurred, the movement of molecules in the air ceased, because diversity was necessary to potential, and potential was necessary for activity, i.e., the conversion to kinetic energy.

To summarize: Just as any other assumption, mechanism -- the theory of absolute physical order-- required supporting data before gaining wide acceptance in the scientific community. In this regard, any data which showed possible exceptions to mechanism was taken seriously. Life appeared to be an exception. However, Darwin's theories of descent and natural selection suggested that life forms developed according to material laws. Human consciousness was a second and possible exception. However, parallelism suggested that it could be explained through observing chemical reactions in the brain. Finally, the total activity of the universe was discovered to be subject to the physical laws of thermodynamics.

For science the chief implication of mechanism is that occurrences in the universe are both predictable and explainable. Nothing is totally unique, and nothing is an exception to absolute order. Ultimately everything can be described as 'blind' adherence to the material laws; to ask their meaning is not relevant.

Mechanism, which was characteristic of science, was also to be found within the philosophies of this period. In the late nineteenth and early twentieth centuries, when moving from the area of science into the field of philosophy, the term 'materialism' is used in place of mechanism. That is, philosophers tended to call men of science mechanists -- but others in their own field of philosophy, holding mechanistic views, were referred to as materialists.

The term 'spiritualism', for example, might mean the opposite of either mechanism or materialism. Materialism in the middle to the late nineteenth century was the philosophic position which held that all activity can be explained by the potential already present within matter. This clearly makes it consistent with a physics which explains all motion in terms of potential and kinetic energy. It is opposed to any form of spiritualism which would posit an extra-material force working upon matter. The three philosophical forms of mechanism were evolutionism, atomism, and secondary causality or historical determinism. We will now introduce these three topics.

The term evolution was actually a philosophical term prior to Darwin. As a pre-Darwinian philosophical concept it was an example of materialism, because evolution was understood as the gradual unfolding of what was already possible within matter. The philoso-

5

phical concept of evolution as an unfolding of matter's
potential was most influentially put forward by
Herbert Spencer in FIRST PRINCIPLES.8

Along with a mechanistic interpretation of evolution we will comment on two other ways of expressing
a belief in a materialistic philosophy. First, atomism
is what one might call the 'classic' statement of
materialism. The principle characteristic of all forms
of atomism is the assumption that there exists an
absolutely smallest material particle, which is not
subject to further division. As Ward says, "Thus,
in spite of the etymological identity of atom and
individual, pluralism has nothing in common with
atomism beyond the bare fact that both recognize a
many; for the atom is credited with no spontaneity and
is completely determined from without."9 In other
words, it is the atom, functioning according to the
physical laws, which ultimately determines the course
of events.

The third of the materialistic philosophies might
well be described as historical determinism or secondary causality. This form of mechanism is illustrated
by a position which assumes that "...beyond humanity
and history, beyond, if you will, the whole realm of
sentient life, nature is there all the while, and
there as no mere background but as the basis of the
whole, the fundamental plasma which can only be shaped
because it is itself determinate and orderly."10

Nature is assumed to be a mechanistic whole quite
apart from any consideration of what man is able to
know specifically about that whole. Furthermore, one
might suggest that the concept of 'ether', i.e. the
medium or plasma in which activity occurs, a concept
re-popularized in the nineteenth century, also comes
under this form of mechanism. Put in another way,
extension is believed to be the only primary quality,
and all other qualities are secondary.

Our discussion of materialistic philosophy would
not be complete without mentioning the concepts of

6

teleology and finalism. Scientific mechanism is non-teleological. That is, it refuses to admit that the activity in the world is purposeful in any ultimate sense. The laws of nature are not working toward any observable goal. What may appear to be purposefulness in a particular situation is relative only to that situation, and not to the whole.

We might, on the other hand, assume that a philosophy which proposed a teleological position would not be mechanistic. However, Bergson points out that this is not the case with 'finalism'. Both finalism and mechanism proceed on the assumption of a pre-established order. Scientific mechanism has merely eliminated the anthropomorphic, i.e. ontological, character of most finalism, and has gotten rid of the end pursued.11

Finalism could well be illustrated by the belief that in retrospect one can see the human species as representing the very organism which the entire evolutionary process was destined to create. At every stage in the process natural selection was acting to preserve just those structures which would make for the highest possible life form -- man. In other words, the evolutionary stages demonstrated a teleological aspect implicit within the natural laws. This purpose might well be understood by the term 'progress'.

Each of our examples of materialistic philosophy, i.e., evolutionism, atomism, historical determinism and finalism are developments in philosophy that are associated with scientific mechanism. They all conclude that the key to understanding the material reality rests in seeing that universal order is the result of some abstract principle inherently incorporated by matter. This abstract principle is absolute because it remains the same in every relation possible. As the absolute principle is innate to matter, men, who are themselves grounded in material reality, have no source of information about an absolute principle which is independent of material reality.

7

Metaphysics is that branch of philosophy which is associated with an attempt to comprehend the universe as a whole. And furthermore its aim is to achieve as precise a conception as possible. If one accepts this definition of the aim of metaphysics, this aim would appear to be totally satisfied by mechansim. Mechanism is a way of understanding the universe in terms of a single unifying principle. The laws of nature, functioning without exception, and applicable in all situations, are a very precise explanation of how the universe holds together.

It would seem that mechanism answered philosophy's call for an explanation of the universe. As mechanism's explanation is wholly physical, the aim of metaphysics seems to be achieved without the need of a metaphysics -- of going beyond the physical. If science had successfully ended metaphysical speculation Process philosophy would never have developed. (Process has a definite metaphysics.) However, metaphysics refused to die. As we will see in Chapter II, where we consider the topic of 'vitalism', there continued to be substantial speculation on the idea that scientific evidence showed 'life' as an exception to the physical laws. The debate between mechanism and vitalism is a contributing factor to the development of modern Process.

Before moving to the topic of vitalism, it is important to note an interesting connection between some vitalisms and the mechanism we have been discussing. In moving beyond the physical, animists or vitalists do not necessarily deny mechanism's belief in a universal order. Instead they may merely argue that the source of order is outside of the material realm, and is not innate to matter.

In speaking of the order to the universe, we are referring to the organization of 'activity'. According to mechanism activity is inherently contained in matter, and is organized in terms of material structure. On the other hand, some animisms and vitalisms argue that the activity of living organism is not an activity organized according to the same plan as the activity of dead matter. If this latter contention is supported, then the two most likely conclusions are: (1) that matter represents one kind of activity and life another, or (2) that a single source of activity, outside of matter, can account for the organization of both matter and life.

The first option clearly suggests a dualism between physical and metaphysical activity. The second option supposes a single metaphysical source of activity. This single metaphysical source would be absolute in the sense that it unifies all reality on the basis of activity. As it would be contradictory to speak of a unity 'outside' of the absolute principle, unity must take place within the principle of activity. Furthermore, given the fact that the metaphysical order is absolute, the physical order must be determined by the metaphysical order.

Based upon such reasoning McDougall, for example, says that material order reflects a divine or spiritual order. This spiritual order is not innate to matter but works upon matter. However, this amounts to saying that while activity is indeed more complex than mechanism allows, it is nevertheless ultimately deterministic because it is unified throughout.

The point is that vitalism may have an understanding of activity which is very different from the meaning of the term in mechanism, and yet arrive at a determinism parallel to materialistic determinism. It is this point that we wish to understand fully, because it is the key to the next step in the development of Process.

1 Ward, James. THE REALM OF ENDS OR PLURALISM AND THEISM. (Cambridge: The University Press, 1911). p.4.
2 McDougall, William. BODY AND MIND. (London: Methuen, 1911). p. 48.

3 Driesch, Hans. THE SCIENCE AND PHILOSOPHY OF ORGAN-
    ISM. (London: Adams and Charles Black, 1908).
    Vol. I, p. 290.
4 ibid. Vol. I, p. 283.
5 Bergson, Henri. MATTER AND MEMORY. trans. Nancy
    Margaret Paul and W. Scott Palmer. (London:
    Swan Sonnenschein, 1911). p. xi.
6 Haldane, J.S. MECHANISM, LIFE AND PERSONALITY.
    (London: John Murry, 1913). p. 28.
7 Ward. THE REALM OF ENDS. p. 9.
8 Spencer, Herbert. FIRST PRINCIPLES. (London:
    Williams & Norgate, 1870). Third Edition.
9 Ward. THE REALM OF ENDS. p. 51.
10 ibid. p. 20.
11 Bergson, Henri. CREATIVE EVOLUTION. trans., Arthur
    Mitchell. (London: Macmillan, 1911). pp. 94-100.

CHAPTER II

VITALISM AND ANIMISM

Vitalism is the belief that the activity of organisms cannot be totally explained by a mechanistic theory, which holds that activity is innate to matter and is ordered according to the material structure. Instead vitalism holds that activity can be fully explained only by the introduction of some extra-material structure. Under the general category of vitalistic will come a wide variety of thinkers who hold very different positions. Nevertheless, the above definition of vitalism holds generally true.

In Chapter I we mentioned that the strengthening of the mechanistic position resulted from three areas of scientific achievement: (1) a mechanistic explanation for adaptation, (2) a mechanistic account of the nervous system, (3) the formulation of the laws of thermodynamics. We will begin our study of vitalism by considering why leading vitalists attempted to call into question the conclusions which developed out of these developments.

In the late nineteenth and early twentieth century the issue of vitalism was the issue of the 'uniqueness of life'. The chief question was whether or not the phenomenon of the activity of life could be explained by a purely mechanistic formulation. Certain men, many of whom were students of biology, said that life could not be explained mechanistically.

'Epigenesis' is a position which sees evolution as producing 'more than' the potential already present in matter. The German biologist and philosopher Hans Driesch was a leading advocate of epigenesis. He presents three, from his viewpoint conclusive, arguments against the concept that a living organism is merely a machine.1

The first of these three proofs is based on

11

discoveries that he made in the area of individual morphogenesis. The cells of certain life forms in at least the second and third stages of cell division, were, he discovered, 'harmonious-equipontential systems'. This term means that, if the cells after their initial divisions are separated, each new cell demonstrates the potential of developing into a full organism (of sometimes reduced size). Driesch says,

> Therefore, there can be neither any sort of causality based upon constellation underlying the differentation of harmonious-equipotential systems. For a machine, typical with regard to the three chief dimensions of space, cannot remains itself if you remove parts of it or if you rearrange its parts at will.[2]

As we have already indicated, vitalism supposes that some extra-material source of activity must account for the activity of organisms, e.g., harmonious-equipotential systems. Driesch chooses to call this force an 'entelechy'. The term entelechy came into wide use among vitalists.

The fact of heredity is Driesch's second proof for vitalism. Perhaps from a modern viewpoint, it would be clearer to call this a proof based upon the process of sexual reproduction. Indeed, most of the modern information about genetic heredity was unknown to Driesch. The point concerning reproduction is that it comes about by cell division. Nevertheless, the result of this division is a whole organism essentially like the parent organisms. No machine, says Driesch, is able to go through a series of divisions and remain what it is.

Driesch's third proof is a refutation of the purely mechanistic functioning of the nervous system. In the widest sense Driesch argues that the response of individuals does not directly correspond to a given stimulus. For example, Driesch argues that no machine

12

is capable of spontaneous regeneration of organs; nor can a machine respond with anything similar to the development of antibodies by the blood of living organisms. To account for the ability of organisms to make unique response to stimuli Driesch posits the existence of forces that he names 'psychoids'.

While these three proofs are central to the biological refutation of the traditional understanding of evolution as an 'unfolding', we have not made any direct mention of Darwin's theory of adaptation by natural selection. The reason is that Driesch held that the science of his day did not know enough about adaptation to use it as a proof either for or against vitalism. He believed that accurate knowledge was limited in biology to some information about individual morphogenesis. Of adaptation he says, "Morphological adaptation is no part of individual morphogenesis proper, but occurs previous to the full individual life of an organism, previous to its full functional life; for it relates to the functions of the complete organism."3

Henri Bergson in CREATIVE EVOLUTION makes two additional observations concerning biology's ignorance about how adaptation occurs. First he says that a mechanistic adaptation should produce increasingly perfect harmony among organisms. However, this is not the case. Adaptation appears to be something which promotes individuality.4

Bergson's second observation is that many biologists of his day continued to interpret evolution as if the Aristotelian hypothesis, that vegetative, instinctive and rational life represent three successive degrees of development, was supported by modern evidence. Bergson argues that the difference among these three is not "a difference of intensity, nor, more generally, of degree, but of kind."5

Having looked at the vitalists' refutation of mechanistic evolution through natural selection, we will consider their response to the theory of the

13

conservation of energy and of entropy. Driesch himself
says that his 'entelechy' avoids entropy. Like many
other thinkers, he does not say that the theory of
entropy is wrong altogether; rather it is not adequate
to include all reality -- it is avoided by life.

Driesch says that entropy is an explanation appropriate to energy. But, entelechy is not a form of
energy. Driesch bases this conclusion on a definition
of entropy as being the impossibility of an increase
in the degree of manifoldness, i.e., of complexity or
order. 6

Manifoldness implies that there is a corresponding
increase in potential. For example, in the case of the
harmonious-equipotential system, described by Driesch,
each cell appears to have a potential to form a total
organism. The more complex the organism becomes, the
greater the corresponding potential within each cell.
Life with its increasingly complex organization would
appear to be creating energy. Driesch does not say
that entelechy increases energy. What he does say is
that entelechy is non-energetic. Therefore, instead
of an increase in potential energy, he believes that
something new has been introduced. According to
thermodynamics, this interpretation would not avoid
the issue that nothing new can be introduced into the
system.

Bergson's position on entropy is characteristic
of his essentially dualistic view of matter and life.
In his own words: "In vital activity we see, then, that
which subsists of the direct movement in the inverted
movement, a reality which is making itself in reality
which is unmaking itself."7

What is characteristic of life, says Bergson, is
its being able to accumulate energy and to redirect it
without expending energy. He says "...Life has a
tendency to accumulate in a reservoir, as do especially
the green parts of vegetables, with a view to an
instantaneous discharge, like that which an animal
brings about..."8 In this sense entropy is not

overcome necessarily, but it is clearly retarded.
Such activity lead Bergson to adopt vitalism, because
he sees in life a conscious effort to overcome the
general laws of inert matter.

These arguments for vitalism did not cause
scientists to flock into the camp. By in large the
scientific community considered them weak. These
arguments did arouse the interest of some philosophers.
Vitalism became a basis for certain philosophical
positions that posited the necessity of some 'vital
force' outside or along with the material order.

Bergson suggested that the source of vital
activity, his so-called 'elan vital', may be a new
kind of energy. Bergson points out that Leibniz
developed his philosophy on the basis of kinetic
energy alone. Only later was the concept of potential
energy added as a necessary adjunct. In like manner,
one might suppose a new kind of energy which is
necessary in order to account for the activity of life.
This necessary elan, says Bergson, is transmitted by
heredity in the same way as the other characteristics
of the organism. He considers elan to be a burst of
pure energy. The source of this pure energy one may
wish to call God. Matter represents the decay of this
pure potential.

Driesch finally turns his entelechy into a vital
force. Eventhough he insists that it is a non-
energetic force. Driesch persists in calling the
entelechy 'It". It is eternal. It is neither matter
nor energy. It is not subject to space and time. In
short, he says, It is a teleological factor within
the universe.9

For yet another thinker, William McDougall, it is
appropriate to call the vital force 'mind' rather than
spirit or energy. Mind says McDougall is a non-
physical reality. It acts upon matter, and is not in
any way the result of the material world. By this
statement he rejects any idea that mind depends for
its existence upon matter. Furthermore, if one

prefers, as McDougall himself sometimes does, the word 'soul'
may be used in place of mind.10

This post-Darwinian vitalism is often called Neo-
vitalism. At least that was the designation assigned
to it in the early twentieth century. The most significant characteristics of neo-vitalism, in terms of its
influence on the development of Process, was that it
profoundly reopened the issue of individuality. In a
purely mechanistic system concepts such as individuality, novelty, freedom, creativeness, purpose and becoming have no really ultimate meaning. In a vitalistic
system, however, this is not the case.

Vitalism, as we have been discussing it, is
necessarily pluralistic in several respects. Pluralism
the vitalists argue is essential in order to explain
vital activity. Of course, the chief dilemma for
pluralism is how to account for the apparent unity
admitting diversity. The effort to do just this was
a second task of neo-vitalism. Undoubtedly the most
comprehensive statement concerning pluralism and unity
was James Ward's PLURALISM AND THEISM.

It should be quite clear that the theory of
mechanism is the theory of an order, or of laws, that
predetermine the entire universe, and eliminate true
diversity. Ward points out that there are unique acts
and deeds that have their origin in the individual
centers of experience, i.e., in individual minds. 11
For example, Ward argues that value is not intrinsic
to nature, but value results from the individual's
attitudes and interests.

It is most especially in the field of biology
that Ward sees proof of individuality. For example,
among life forms there is real evidence of diversity.
Plants, the lower animals, and man -- in their present
forms -- are not products of a single line of development, but he says, are cases of actual diversity; of
a true multiplicity of forms. Adaptation also
appears to Ward to act according to the particular
organism, rather than universally. Finally, that fact

16

called entropy, which life is able to avoid, allows
life to show its diversity. These are, of course,
all ideas borrowed from neo-vitalism.

Ward believes that individualization is the chief
fact of history. Individuality, he felt, is more and
more apparent as one moves to the higher life forms.
Furthermore, Ward says that progress can only be
defined as an interaction of a plurality of individuals.12

Bergson, equally influenced by neo-vitalism, joins
Ward in the argument for individuality. In his TIME
AND FREE WILL Bergson uses a more physiological approach for the proof of individuality. Here he points to
a large number of experiments which disprove parallelism. In Chapter I we discussed parallelism as the
position that brain states are parallel to chemical
reactions. Now Bergson wants to argue that mental
states are not totally predictable.

Bergson's most powerful argument against parallelism and for pluralism is his concept of 'time'.
Generally philosophers of his day believed that one of
Bergson's greatest achievements was his particular
introduction of the concept of time into philosophy.
Time, he says, is a reality accepted by physical
science. Yet the very concept of time is a refutation
of the mechanistic explanation of the universe. For
he points out that if all reality is programmed, as
finalism supposes, time is a useless concept.13

He further says that, in establishing their mathematical (mechanical) laws, scientists select a
hypothetical point. Based upon this point they make
measurements and construct their theories. Time in the
sense of 'duration', however, cannot be explained as a
single point. Rather, a series of points is necessary
in order to account for the movement of time. That
time does so move, and that this movement has meaning,
can be proven by the simple fact that a man grows
older.

For the fact of evolution to have taken place, says Bergson, one must assume a persistence of the past into the present. That is, there must be a hyphen or connecting link between points.14 Thus in accepting time we accept plurality.

For Ward history becomes the unity of individuals. A common history provides the background in which individuals function. What do we share in common? 'A history.' In spite of the common elements of this history, it is composed of a plurality of individuals intent on self-betterment as well as self-conservation. History is a medium which not only allows, but also assumes diversity.

Bergson, again in a more scientific vein, talks of time rather than history. Time is a persistence of the past -- the common past -- into the present. Time is also a connecting link among diverse parts. Time would not exist if there was no diversity. Time is the medium in which diversity exists. The whole of the past is brought into every present moment.

This concept of time or history as the medium of unity is a key factor, as we will see, in the development of Process thought. However, Bergson introduces this factor to support the hypothesis that in order for activity to take place one must assume a multiplicity. He illustrates his point primarily in terms of life. Indeed, we must remember that Bergson associates activity with life alone. Entropy, inactivity, is the characteristic state of matter.

Bergson further holds that, in life forms, feelings are the root of activity. A feeling, says Bergson, is not a unity but a complexity. In TIME AND FREE WILL Bergson says that science has proven that the intensity of a feeling is directly related to the multiplicity of simple states, which consciousness dimly discerns within the total feeling.15 For example the intensity of a pain is determined by the number of pain-sensative nerves affected. There is no other way of explaining intensity within conscious states.

Thus consciousness of itself demands the reality of a multiplicity.

From a scientific viewpoint, vitalism suggests that the phenomenon of life is an exception to the principle that all activity is organized in terms of material structure. This means that the absoluteness of the physical laws cannot be maintained. Althought there was a tendency among vitalists to accept that the physical laws were absolute when applied only to 'dead' matter.

In the hands of philosophers vitalistic conclusions suggested that life was unlike matter, in that only the former demonstrated true individuality or multiplicity. The concept of 'true' individuality or multiplicity includes the idea that the activity of entities is not determined. Materialism demonstrated that the activity of matter was determined by its structure. In other words the organization of activity was built-in. However, as we have just seen, material structure did not appear to fully account for the activity of living organisms. Pushed to an extreme, vitalism could be used to support the rejection of any concept of absolute order, in favor of an ultimate pluralism.

The Process thinkers who we will be considering in the next several Chapters are not prepared to ignore the implications of either mechanism or vitalism. On the one hand they will attempt to confront the issue of multiplicity being necessary to the activity of life. On the other hand they will see that it is also necessary to address mechanism's conclusion that some absolute principle orders or unifies all reality. The problem will be to formulate a cosmology in which both order and diversity -- unity and multiplicity -- have a place.

The apparent contradictions that life posed to an ordered universe were not the direct concern of the biologists who provided the scientific foundations for vitalism. However, these were a concern for the philosophers who were seeking a metaphysics. Metaphysics seeks comprehensiveness. It had to either accept some form of pluralism, or discount vitalistic data, or formulate some principle of activity that by some inner necessity is the same in relation to both matter and also life; this principle of activity would then be absolute. It is in part the effort within metaphysices to find a principle of activity for both matter and life that caused the concept of a process to begin to take shape.

The above discussion also indicates that Process began as a search for a new metaphysics. It began as a search for a metaphysics that could respond fully to the discoveries of modern science. Our next step must be a consideration of how selected philosophers conducted this search, and the conclusions that they reached.

1 Driesch generally uses the word machine in a chemical sense. 'A machine' is a typical configuration of physical and chemical constituents, by the action of which a typical effect is attained.
2 Driesch. PHILOSOPHY OF ORGANISM. Vol. I. p. 141.
3 ibid. p. 142.
4 Bergson. CREATIVE EVOLUTION. p. 53.   5 ibid. p. 142.
6 Driesch, Hans. THE PROBLEM OF INDIVIDUALITY. (London: Macmillan, 1914). pp. 35-36.
7 Bergson. CREATIVE EVOLUTION. p. 261.
8 ibid. p. 260.
9 Driesch. PHILOSOPHY OF ORGANISM. Vol. II. p. 205.
10 McDougall. BODY AND MIND. p. 299.
11 Ward. THE REALM OF ENDS. p. 18.   12 ibid. p. 97.
13 Bergson. CREATIVE EVOLUTION. P.41.   14 ibid. p. 24.
15 Bergson, Henri. TIME AND FREE WILL. trans., F.L. Pogson. (London: Swan Sonnenschein, 1910). pp. 31-32.

CHAPTER III

F.H. BRADLEY'S ABSOLUTISM

F.H. Bradley's work is a good place to begin our discussion about how the factors of unity and diversity, as presented by materialism and vitalism, can be reconciled. His position is that neither system answers the dilemma. Indeed he holds that the solution must be reached on a metaphysical level. Of course, he agrees that both materialiam and vitalism have specific insights that are of use to metaphysics.

Bradley's book APPEARANCE AND REALITY was one of the first to make clear that the issues between materialism and vitalism point to a central problem for modern metaphyscis. His works also have the advantage of clearly illustrating the factors involved. Therefore, while his conclusions are not always consistent with Process thinking, it is appropriate to begin with him.

The physical world, says Bradley, 'appears' to us as a multiplicity -- a world of many values in which no value seems to be able to involve all the rest. 1 Yet we do not comprehend the world as simply piecemeal or by fragments, but somehow as a whole. Like an exponent of mechanism, Bradley believes that whatever unifies the cosmos must be absolute. Yet he cannot see how materialism justifies its belief that it can explain this unity or order by a physical principle. Thus he says that the explanation of the absolute order is a topic for metaphysics.

He uses many examples of the inadequacy of attempts by materialists to discover the cosmic principle of unity within the physical world. For example, he points out that the concept of time, which was often credited as proving unity, was in fact not able to do so. Time says Bradley is within the mind. This means that time is relative to mind. And he says, what we are looking for in the principle of unity is something which relates -- not a relationship. Time is a mere relationship, used as that which relates.

For Bradley the 'Absolute' is that which relates, but in itself is free from relationships. His point that the Absolute is not capable of relating dates to Hegel's treatment of the term Absolute.

Not only did he feel that the materialists were unable to account for unity, but he also believed that religion failed to prove unity metaphysically -- although the spiritual level was, in his mind, where unity could be demonstrated. In his treatment of the "God of Religion" Bradley is especially careful to point out the God cannot be understood as the Absolute. The God of Religion is personal. He has relationships. Therefore, God can only be an appearance of the true Absolute.[2]

Nevertheless, the fact of unity remains a reality quite apart from the situation that we have only been able to account for appearances of it. Bradley concludes, therefore, that we must say that unity is nothing other than an experience. "It will hence be a single all-inclusive experience, which embraces every partial diversity in concord."[3]

At this point the way is opened for another understanding of the term absolute. It does not in Bradley's work refer to an abstract physical principle. Instead, the term refers to an actual concrete unity of the complexities, and even contradictions, of reality. This understanding is validated by experience. Experience itself is a whole; yet it is composed of many contradictions. However, says Bradley, if these contradictions remain unresolved, then there could be no permanence. And permanence is demanded because there is change.

Bradley admits to change and diversity, and he says that the evolution of life, for example, demonstrates them. At this point he is in agreement with many of the vitalists. Yet he says that vitalism, when it accounts for unity at all, continues to depend

22

upon the material as the ground of permanence. For example, vitalists like Bergson and Driesch insist that some force acts upon the material to create permanence. This action upon the material always takes the form of a relationship; and Bradley's point has been that we are seeking for that which relates rather than a relationship.

Neither mechanism's call for unity nor vitalism's support of plurality is wrong -- but neither can account for both. According to Bradley, therefore, a unified reality cannot be described by any form of materialism or vitalism. He says that we are so limited to appearances that we cannot be sure of the dividing line between the organic and the inorganic. To attempt to prove something on either the basis of matter or organism is useless. Moreover, he says that both vitalism and mechanism tend to assume that matter came before mind. However, matter -- the whole of nature -- is nothing other than a category of mind. Without the action of mind nature does not exist. Mind or experience supplies the unity to nature. Unity, in this sense, is metaphysical.

Bradley often chooses to speak of the metaphysical as the 'spiritual'. In talking about the spiritual, it is important to keep in mind Bradley's distinction between religion and metaphysics. Religion for Bradley deals with relationships -- especially morals. The establishment of morals he says is a valuable task for religion. Metaphysics deals with the Absolute. He concludes, "I can enter here no further on this matter than to express my opinion that to invade the region of philosophy is contrary to the interests of a sound morality or religion."4

From the spiritual or metaphysical level mind gives the experience of wholeness to reality. Apart from this experience of wholeness unity cannot be established rationally. There is in the material world neither a clear reason for unity nor diversity. If we attempt to establish unity in matter we simply deal with relationships. The laws which are said to

relate matter are not within the material, but are
imposed upon the material by the mind.

Apparently the world of matter is merely a diversity; lacking unity until the mind imposes it -- in
the form of laws or ideas. Bradley quickly admits
that this theory makes all of our sensual experience
about the material world illusory. We do experience
the material world as having a unity within itself.
Here is, in general, the greatest problem for his
system; the material world must be accepted as lacking
any organized reality in itself.

Are we then to assume that sensual experience is
meaningless? Here Bradley says no. Somehow our sense
impressions, although they are mere appearances, must
have meaning. What this meaning is does not become
clear, except that it is a meaning to be resolved only
on the spiritual level.

Bradley believes that he has eliminated the possibilities of solving the riddle of the ultimate truth
of materialism or vitalism. For him the Absolute,
that which relates, must be completely separated from
the material world. Unity is a metaphysical concept.

Turning the world into a realm of mere appearances was a position that most philosophers of the
period were unwilling to accept. Nevertheless, a few
of Bradley's points are important to the development
of Process. First, Bradley saw that the sciences,
rather than doing away with the need for metaphysics,
were actually opening new possibilities for philosophy.
Process is a metaphysical response to some of the very
issues addressed by Bradley. Second, Bradley saw that
the determinism of modern materialism called for a
philosophical response rather than a religious one.
Religion, he observed, was not in a position to
respond to science. The battleground was not science
vs. religion; rather it was metaphysics vs. materialism. Process thought is a metaphysics for the era of
modern science. Most important of all Bradley introduced a new understanding of the term 'absolute.' The

24

Absolute is something which allows and even depends
upon   diversity.

Let us consider this last point. The experience
of wholeness, whatever else it might be, is a metaphysical imposition of unity -- that imposition being
made by mind. However, there must also exist a true
diversity upon which the unity is imposed. That
which relates does not preclude the necessity of
relata. Indeed it depends upon them. The activity of
the universe depends on something that relates and on
relata. They cannot be the same thing. This is in
general agreement with later Process thought.

Our next two Chapters will, in a sense, be a step
backwards from Bradley's level of Process thinking.
He assumed that neither mechanism nor vitalism could
solve the problems of unity and diversity. However,
there were certain vitalists who attempted to make
vitalism do just that. As Bradley might have predicted,
they were not very successful. Nevertheless, their
efforts uncovered certain conclusions that finally
contributed to a clearer statement of a Process
position. In Chapters IV and V we will be looking at
some of the attempts to show that a predominately
vitalistic position can account for the apparent unity
in the cosmos.

1 Bradley, F.H. APPEARANCE AND REALITY. (London:
        George Allen & Unwin, 1916). p. 30.
2 ibid. p. 448.   3 ibid. p. 147.
4 Bradley, F.H. ESSAYS ON TRUTH AND REALITY. (Oxford:
        The Clarendon Press, 1914). p. 11.

26

CHAPTER IV

NEO-VITALISM

Henri Bergson and Hans Driesch have already been introduced to the reader as vitalists. In many respects they share similar positions. In part the reason is that both of their positions use the language of biology. However, modern biology was in its infancy. One must be sensative to the relatively primitive state of that science as compared with early twentieth century physics.

Indeed, from today's point of view most of the proofs for vitalism were negative. That is, the conclusions were chiefly the results of inadequate experimental techniques or inferior equipment. Vitalism was a possible explanation for what could not be prove experimentally in biology; but truly positive evidence for vitalism was woefully lacking. Yet Bergson and Driesch, in their efforts to establish vitalism, made important strides toward outlining a Process position. Let us consider the work of these thinkers again.

In his ADVENTURES OF IDEAS the Process thinker Alfred North Whitehead says, "The point which is here relevant, is that the zest of human adventure presupposes for its material a scheme of things with a worth beyond any single occasion."1 In spite of many particular differences between the thought of Whitehead and Bergson, the foregoing quotation captures extremely well an essential formulation introduced in great part by Bergson's writings. Bergson would use the word 'state' rather than 'occasion', but his point would be the same. The real, as we know it, argues Bergson, appears to be made up of separate flashes that are independent of each other; yet value must be understood in terms of continuity. He therefore tries to show that the vital principle, which is used to argue against mechanism in favor of true diversity, also provides the scheme of unity behind diversity. Thus he hopes to answer the need for unity and

27

diversity within a single system.

The key to Bergson's solution lies in his understanding of the nature of 'activity'. Activity, he
says, is composed of both plurality and unity. The
name that he gives to activity is 'elan vital', which
we have already mentioned. Elan does not simply
presuppose relationships. It is that which both
relates and also has relationships. Our earlier
discussions of entropy clearly illustrated this point.
In those discussions we discovered that when diversity
ceases, activity ceases. Because diversity in essential to activity.

The fact that life has activity presupposes
diversity and unity. Yet mechanism, according to
Bergson, attempts to deny diversity through the unity
of its material forms and laws. Mechanists tried to
make laws absolute; thus eliminating the possibility
of diversity. Unity cannot be explained, therefore,
by physical laws. There can be, as Bradley suggested,
no 'intellectual' explanation for unity.2

What does account for unity, according to
Bergson, is 'intuition'. Intuition, he says, is of
the common elan, which is not mechanistic. Our intuition is the experience of diversity within unity.
Here again Bradley and Bergson appear to be in agreement. Both conclude that unity must be imposed on
matter. Unity is not built into material reality.
Nature of itself is a diversity which only conscious
experience can make into a unity. Intuition, according
to Bergson, takes us into the very center of reality.
In experience we discover duration. "Duration" is
characterized by a past that swells into a present
that is absolutely new.3

According to Bergson the intuition exists in company with the 'intellect'. Intellect, like
intuition, imposes unity upon nature. Intuition, however, experiences unity as duration, while intellect
experiences 'repetition'. In each new generation
characteristics are modified, but repetition seems also

to be essential to the physical order. In fact, heredity, which is activity, is characterized by process. However, in matter, where true activity is not present, repetition appears as cause and effect. Seeing cause and effect in matter, intellect expects to see cause and effect in heredity. It is a mistake of intellect to impose cause and effect upon living organisms. Intuition overcomes this error through its experience of duration -- process.

The first characteristic of Process philosophy demonstrated by vitalism is the belief that activity is made up of both unity and diversity. Now we can observe a second characteristic; namely, the conviction that activity requires the existence of what Bergson calls 'mind'. For it is only in mind that the two elements of activity are truly present.

The problem which most philosophers had with Bergson's metaphysics was its strong dualistic implications. Mind and matter appear as categorically non-compatible. Mind is the source of all activity, and matter is entropic. Certain of the vitalistic Process thinkers are going to mediate this dualism.

No explicit reference has been made to the term absolute in our presentation of Bergson's position. This was intentional,as at this point it is better for us to draw a few implicit conclusions. Bergson must agree with Bradley that the material laws are not absolute. Unity cannot be explained by reference to these. The best candidate for Bergson's absolute is activity itself. However, this supports dualism. Matter is excluded from activity under Bergson's view, and would thereby be excluded from absolute unity.

William James finds one aspect of Bergson's dualism helpful; namely, the dualism of intellect and intuition. James in A PLURALISTIC UNIVERSE applauds Bergson, because of what James calls the conclusive refutation of the intellect in favor of felt experience. Indeed the emphasis upon feelings will become an important theme in all Process thought.

In his proofs of vitalism's ability to establish
the unity of nature Hans Driesch has a number of ideas
in common with Bergson. For example, his psychoids
are similar in function to Bergson's minds. That is
the psychoids direct organisms. (Sometimes psychoids
are understood as included in the term entelechy.)
Also, like Bergson, Driesch understands that the vital
force, or source of activity, must somehow be consistent with unity and diversity. Yet he realizes the
logical problem in suggesting that entelechy is something that can remain the same if it is divided into
parts to form a diversity. Thus he suggests that one
must simply accept that the wholeness of entelechy is
not destroyed in spite of observed divisions among
organic bodies.5 Again the intellectual explanation
for unity is denied.

Again we see vitalism's dualistic problem. From
Driesch's position one must assume that entelechy itself is somehow one thing, and its manifestations
within organisms another. This must also mean that
the medium in which it is manifested, i.e., the
substance of the organism, is somehow distinct from
entelechy.

In an attempt to avoid dualism Driesch introduces
his concept of 'becoming'. He says, "The definition --
and the only strict definition -- of the concept of
Nature is, that Nature is a something which satisfies
the postulates of a rational theory of becoming, and
which behaves at the same time as if it were independent and self-persistent in itself."6

Here is a real difference from Bergson's position.
Nature, which for Driesch is a matter-energy reality,
shares becoming with entelechy. For Bergson nature or
matter is devolution. Driesch suggests that all
reality participates in becoming. The problem is that
Driesch's above formulation ignores all regressions,
in favor of a necessary progression.

Perhaps this problem will be clearer if we look
at what Driesch means by the term becoming. His chief

30

illustration of becoming is a Bergsonian concept.--
memory understood as duration, i.e. the constant movement of the past into the present.

Bergson, we may recall, says that memory is a
present unity formed by a past plurality of events.
Thus for memory events form an organized whole. This
organization is a result of memory's participation
in intuition; and it is not an aspect of the material
world given to memory. Although the intellect would
try to convince us that the latter is the case. The
material world, according to Bergson, lacks activity,
i.e. true unity combined with true diversity. Thus
the organization of memory is always more than the
events which seem to compose it.

Driesch, on the other hand, holds that the form
taken by memory is in fact a legitimate model for
nature. With regard to nature, Driesch says, one can
pick out a particular It which endures, and connect
the changes that occur in any It. Likewise, memory
has that which endures as well as that which changes.
A natural system according to Driesch can increase in
complexity, i.e., manifoldness, and yet retain an
essential identity. His classic example is the
'organism'. In his major work PROCESS AND REALITY
Whitehead refers to his own work as a 'philosophy of
organism'. The concept of organism adopted by Process
can in part be traced to the spirit of the following
concepts presented by Driesch.

In the sense of organism, Driesch says, all of
nature is more than a mere sum of elementary concepts.
Natural systems do demonstrate a manifoldness not
unlike that of Bergson's memory. It is this organic
manifoldness -- a category of wholeness -- which
Driesch means by the term becoming. In some degree
all of reality is organic. Becoming, however, is not
built into nature.

In his PHILOSOPHY OF ORGANISM Driesch refers to
becoming in nature as a 'window into the absolute.'7
The discussion indicates that Driesch equates becoming

31

with entelechy and then suggests that entelechy is
absolute. Absoluteness is understood as organic,
and the organism becomes the model for the entire
universe. The dualistic nature of vitalism is thus
avoided by excluding nothing from the concept of an
organism.

Yet Driesch does not completely avoid dualism.
He has argued that activity, becoming, is an organic
principle. As an organic principle it includes all of
reality. However, if this organic principle, also
called entelechy, is absolute, Driesch is never able
to explain how entelechy remains a whole in spite of
its division into parts. Furthermore, entelechy
does not seem to be the same as the matter-energy
reality. Clearly this means that entelechy and the
matter-energy reality have aspects that are outside of
the common becoming. Dualism is not completely
avoided. Of course it makes sense to say that matter
and life have something in common, but simply having
something in common may not be enough to account for
unity in a strict sense.

Thus we must conclude that neither Bergson nor
Driesch was able to show that vitalism could explain
absolute cosmic unity, while allowing for diversity.
On the other hand, they have demonstrated that the
concept of cosmic unity may not be nearly as simple as
materialism was led to believe. What was long clear
to philosophy, now becomes apparent in some fields of
science; namely, that the implications of absolute
unity are not easily reconciled with a demand for a
true diversity.

On the positive side, their concept that the
existence of activity, which was so much taken for
granted by the physical sciences, is itself difficult
to reconcile with the implications of materialism will
grow in importance as we continue the survey of how
Process develops. Physics was so concerned to show
that the organization of activity followed absolute
physical laws that it neglected to notice that, as
activity never existed apart from diversity, it could

not be innate to matter. Matter of itself lacks true diversity -- and Bradley even suggested that it lacked unity. If not inherently within matter, activity must have another source. Both Bergson and Driesch have suggested that this source is a vital principle that is itself an interaction between unity and diversity. Driesch says that all organisms are characterized by just such an interaction. Thus he suggests that we could think of the entire universe as an organism. This universal organism would be absolute in the sense that it contains all of reality. This is not to suggest, of course, that the cosmic organism has being as well as becoming. Driesch did not consider such a possibility one way or the other.

1 Whitehead, A.N. ADVENTURES OF IDEAS. (Cambridge: University Press, 1933). p. 372.
2 Bergson, Henri. CREATIVE EVOLUTION. P. 160.
3 ibid. p. 210.
4 James, William. A PLURALISTIC UNIVERSE. (London: Longmans, Green, 1901). pp. 258-260.
5 Driesch. PHILOSOPHY OF ORGANISM. Vol. II. p. 258.
6 Driesch, Hans. THE PROBLEM OF INDIVIDUALITY. (London: Macmillan, 1914). p. 45.
7 Driesch. PHILOSOPHY OF ORGANISM. Vol. II. p. 363.

CHAPTER V

SPIRITUAL EVOLUTIONISM

As we have already suggested, vitalistic systems are teleological. That is, they characterize activity in individual organisms as having purposefulness, i.e., activity is not totally predetermined by the material structure. Formulations of this concept, as we have seen, led both Bergson and Driesch into a pluralism -- in at least the sense of dualism.

It is on this point that the thoughts of Ward and Hocking contribute another step to the development of Process. While they do not finally end the dualism in vitalism -- that Process will not be able to accept -- they move further toward resolving Driesch's dilemma of how the vital force can remain a whole in spite of its division into parts. Using Bradley's understanding of the term absolute, as referring to something which unifies all reality by containing it, they will attempt to show that the nature of an absolute cosmic unity is consistent with the relative independence of the parts of such a unity. And indeed that it can have parts. Furthermore, they will adopt something like Driesch's model of the organism for unity.

For Bradley all reality was a mystery, and for Bergson matter remained something of a mystery. It is this sense of unknowing that seems to lead toward dualism. Ward now suggests that a spiritualistic interpretation can eliminate the problem that knowledge of nature is a mystery, and therefore subject to error. In other words, he feels that matter and life can both be known and understood through a spiritualistic interpretation.

By the term 'spiritual' Ward means a unity or harmony which results form increasing individuality. The movement toward harmony, according to Ward, is the only way in which pluralism can account for the reality of unity. Human history is for Ward an example of individuality creating an increasing unity. Ward calls

humanity "the spiritual society."[1] Man is more truly
an individual than any other organism. Yet his level
of social organization is also greatest. This situation Ward calls progressive, because it allows for the
highest possible level of self-betterment.

Organisms that lack social organization tend to
be less successful, and likewise organisms which are
highly organized, but whose members lack individuality
(an ant colony for example), tend not to progress.
Therefore, mankind represents a progress beyond that
of life forms which lack organization or which are
statically organized. Clearly historical progress is
the development of increasing individuality within the
creation of a highly organized society.

Next Ward addresses the question of whether this
spiritual society developed through accident or design.
Ward would answer that it was through design. "The
principle of continuity indeed almost forces us to
posit higher orders of intelligence than our own; and
the fact that we are able to control and modify the
course of evolution suggests that if there are higher
intelligences they can exercise this power in a still
higher degree."[2]

Ward thus agrees that there is a vital force of
some description. However, he insists that this force
could not be described as a mere elan or entelechy.
Rather it must be given an ontological character.
That is, it must have a concrete content, with qualities consistent with creation.

He is now ready to address himself to Bradley's
dilemma of what it is that relates. As we may recall,
Bradley insisted that anything with relationships cannot be that which relates. Ward denies this. He says
that human history proves that the greater the degree
of individuality the greater are the number of relationships. That is, the greater is the unity. This
relatedness is itself the product of increased individuality. If we posit an increasingly individualized
unity, then we must always say that the number of

relationships within the unity increase. If we posit
God, which Ward believes that we must, we posit an
unlimited unity composed of unlimited relationships.
Thus God is the absolute unity who is composed of an
unlimited number of relationships. That which most
relates has the most relationships. God's very unity
also makes individuality possible; just as society
is a unity which makes individualization possible.

Thus Ward makes another step toward Process thought. In the first place, like a vitalist, he argues
that absoluteness cannot be assigned to an abstract
physical principle, because material structure cannot
be the source of vital activity. Second, he understands that unless all activity has a single source,
there is no basis for the unity of the cosmos. Third,
he argues that activity must be absolute since its
inner necessity is a process of individualization.
Fourth, whatever is absolute must have a concrete
content; otherwise concrete reality would not be
included in it, and cosmic unity could not be achieved.
Fifth, he says that the source of activity (creativity)
is an absolute cosmic source -- God --, whose inner
necessity of movement toward harmony is not contrary
to -- but actually promotes -- individualization. Thus
Ward, unlike Bergson (in his sighted works) and
Driesch, gives activity an ontological basis, which
Ward argues allows for 'Becoming'. Vitalistic pluralism results from the vital force not having been
given a concrete ontological basis in the past.

What makes Ward's position different from traditional theism is its strong monistic implications.
The individualization model supposes an absolute
individual who harmonizes all other individuals within
itself. This being the case, we are again at the
conclusion of materialism that absoluteness refers to
an ultimate principle of unity. Ward has merely
accounted for individual purposefulness by suggesting
that the 'absolute' has a purpose, and that it is not
the purposeless absolute physical law of mechanism.
Nevertheless, Ward's point that purpose cannot come
out of purposelessness is an interesting one. It

37

reaffirms philosophy's point that the Absolute must
somehow include purpose, and Ward's understnding of
individualization was helpful in this regard. On the
other hand, Ward does not explain the simple repetition
in the material world, if everything is ordered toward
a progressive harmony.

Ward does not see purpose as a static thing.
Purpose is becoming. It is the creation of greater
unity through greater diversity. Purpose determines
chiefly that the individual shall become more an
individual. Here is another important point that is
also adopted by Process thought. Of course, the point
is clarified and made more strongly by later Process
thinkers. This clarification is needed because Ward's
formulation supposes a rather difficult concept of God.
God seems to be an individual whose individuality is
increased by the greater independence of his parts.

Hocking's work THE MEANING OF GOD IN HUMAN
EXPERIENCE is helpful in establishing a concept of
God which allows for diversity within unity.3 He will
accept the general position put forward by Ward, but
will carry it in a somewhat different direction. He
adds what might be called the 'mystical vision' to a
formulation quite similar to that of Ward's.

Hocking accepts in general the model of individualization for the concept of becoming. That is, he
believes in the reality of a cosmic unity, but he holds
that it is a unity that does not prevent individuality;
it is one that provides for it. Furthermore, he will
accept Ward's position that man is involved in
creativity. Hocking says,

> There are certainly some regions of
> reality which are unfinished. We are
> endowed with wills only because there
> are such regions, to which it is our
> whole occupation to give shape and
> character. In such regions the will-
> to-believe is justified, because it
> is no will-to-make-believe, but a

veritable will to create the
truth in which we believe.4

And what we must believe says Hocking is that all
reality is one. That is, we must believe that individual wills are a part of reality, but also that there
is a reality beyond any particular will. A cosmic
will he argues is the only possible basis for an optimistic view of the universe. To accept plurality
leads to the pessimistic view that harmony can never
be achieved.

Hocking is a monist -- and he would agree to this
title. On the other hand, he is sympathetic to the
position that becoming must be a basic part of reality.
He does not exclude the probability that cosmic unity
employs individual creativity as its working charac-
ter.5   He offers the following summary of monism;

> Monism begins to offer signifi-
> cant basis for our prospects when
> it seizes upon the actual processes
> of the world, and declares that
> they are all cases of One Process.
> In the nature of that One Process
> can be read something of the
> presumable outcome.6

The question of what the outcome will be for the
possibility of becoming is really a new concept.
Ward's position that individualization is the model
for becoming never goes so far as to suggest a final
outcome. Ward simply says that the purpose is
individualization. However, does this mean that man
as we now know him is the conclusion of evolution?
Indeed this seems to be the implication of what Ward
says.

Such a conclusion would not be suprising. The
idea that man is the pinnacle of evolution is a long-
standing concept. Nevertheless, man himself has
changed. Does Ward mean to tell us that man is now at
the end of his evolutionary process? To look at man

as he now is, as the best he will ever be is not a very optimistic picture. Indeed Hocking says, "Optimism, I say, requires this degree of monism; -- belief in an individual Reality, not ourselves, which makes for rightness, and which actually accomplishes rightness when left to its own workings."7

Through the above he suggests that talking about individualization is not enough. Indeed we must be more specific about the nature of individuality. Certainly it is already clear that individuality is composed of both unity and diversity. However, for Hocking this individuality is an 'Ideal' rather than a description of the present condition of man. True individuality must be changeless in the specific sense that it always makes for right.

Absoluteness is the changeless movement toward what is right. True individuality must adopt this aspect of absoluteness, if its purpose is to be understood. To make absoluteless something other than the adoption of the movement toward rightness is to select something unworthy of the concept of absoluteness. Materialism makes such a selection. It selects natural laws as being absolute. Hocking argues that this position leads to mankind's ultimate stagnation. He feels that the closest man comes to a true understanding of the concept of individual is in the mystical experience. That is, the mystic by his conscious effort at super-subjectivity, or super-individualization, reclaims a new increment for the general use.8

In his book Hocking speaks at considerable length in order to describe the mystical experience. Indeed he attempts to show the universal character of this experience through several of the world's religions. In each case he sees that the search for one's self leads to a conclusion of selflessness. The desire to be a true individual ends in the ability to participate in the universal.

When he says 'individual' is an 'ideal', we must not take this to mean that it is abstract. The

40

mystical experience has a real object. The object of
this experience -- also called by Hocking the Object
of Worship -- is a real whole in which all things are
related. It is this whole which makes relationship
possible. Hocking speaks of man as being in pursuit
of the whole. That is, man is in pursuit of becoming
fully individual in the sense of being a part of an
objective whole. To reach this experience of wholeness is the conclusion, the purpose, of the individualization process.

Hocking's work is the last of several attempts
to reconcile the concepts of unity and diversity in a
single vitalistic formulation. Hocking is a vitalist
in the important sense that he sees an active force
qualify the material world. A vitalistic formulation
is one which argues that certain activities of life,
especially purposive self-conscious activity, cannot
be explained by materialism. In other words, vitalism
argues that a material principle of unity cannot be
absolute, as life demonstrates a plurality of forms
inconsistent with material laws.

What has emerged from the discussions up to now
is the insight that on the level of spirit or mind
unity and diversity are complementary, while on the
level of matter they are contradictory. The term
absolute is understood by vitalism to refer to any
unity of diversities. With regard to Bergson's elan,
Driesch's entelechy, Ward's individualization, and
Hocking's mystical experience the development of this
formulation is clearly illustrated.

Behind each of these vitalistic positions is the
assumption that unity and diversity are imposed on the
material world -- at least in part -- by mind. Thus
the reality of matter is not denied. Yet none of these
thinkers satisfactorily explains the fact of matter.
If mind reflects absoluteness, then matter appears to
remain outside of the absolute. Even a complex unity
makes no sense if some aspect of reality is excluded.
The use of the term absolute, as referring to a unity
of all reality, makes most vitalistic formulations

contradictory.

Of course Ward and Hocking profess to be monists.
That is, they argue that matter is not excluded from
the cosmic unity. Matter must somehow fit into God's
plan for harmony. While it is difficult to see how
they support this; let us for a moment suppose it
valid. The necessary implication is that plurality is
not ultimately real. The absolute unity, as a final
harmony, is just as deterministic as the material laws,
understood as an already realized harmony. Although
the former does have the advantage of accounting for
the human experience of disunity, which is one of the
aspects of consciousness that materialism cannot
explain.

Vitalisms give a world view that is emotionally
satisfying to self-conscious beings, but it is unable
to convience all self-conscious beings that its viewpoint is the right one. Therefore, in Chapters VI and
VII we will consider an alternative. The alternative
is an attempt to account for unity and diversity within a materialistic system. This will be an attempt to
demonstrate that the materialistic understanding of
the absoluteness of the physical laws can allow for
the self-conscious experience of plurality.

The vitalists are chiefly important to the
history of Process because they introduced the concept
that activity is a becoming -- a process -- in which
unity and diversity are necessary participants.
Process itself is not a form of vitalism. Nevertheless, vitalistic speculations forced mechanists to
approach their own position in a way that furthered
the development of Process.

1 Ward, James. THE REALM OF ENDS. P. 387.
2 ibid. p. 185.
3 Hocking, William. THE MEANING OF GOD IN HUMAN
        EXPERIENCE. (New Haven: Yale, 1912).
4 ibid. p. 140.   5 pp. 171-172.   6 p. 172.
7 p. 177.   8 p. 404.

CHAPTER VI

NEO-MECHANISM

Vitalistic conclusions, based upon the unique aspects of life, implied that the very fact of activity which required both unity and diversity could not, and was not being explained by the physical laws. Activity could only be understood as a force working through or upon matter. The position of Neo-Mechanism, on the other hand, is that material laws can in fact account for both the unity and diversity required for activity, if they are properly interpreted; and that vitalism is an unsupportable position. Finally the 'new mechanism', as it is sometimes called, admits that other forms of mechanism had encouraged the rise of vitalism by inadequate explanation of the matter-energy relationship.

As we have already said, the vitalists tended to be dualists or monists. This poses a problem for J.S. Haldane. He begins by pointing out that all vitalists want to emphasize the fact of individuality, i.e., true diversity. However, they all end up with some extra-material force that in one way or another controls or animates the organism. This animating force may work blindly and be unconscious as in the case of elan or entelechy; or, the force may be individual, so to speak, and work somehow subconsciously.1

Haldane felt that in his day vitalism was accepted by only a small minority of scientists. But this minority was very vocal. The chief reason for this, he believes, was that much of the experimentation that could have supported mechanism was being inadequately interpreted. Room was always being left for vitalistic conclusions.

Driesch's work is a particular target of Haldane's criticism. This is to be expected as it represents one of the most careful accounts of vitalism; and one that appeared to be supported by a weighty amount of experimental evidence.

Of Driesch's famous proof of entelechy based on the nature of cell division, Haldane says:

> Now there is no evidence at all that each cell, in growing and dividing in the one particular manner which constitutes normal development, is not determined by special physical and chemical stimuli peculiar to its position relatively to the other cells, and to the external environment. We do not yet know what these stimuli are; but probably no physiologist would doubt that they exist, and will be discovered when our methods are fine enough. Hence Driesch's argument for an independent vital force breaks down entirely.[2]

Here we have three objections to vitalism. First, it must assume that no activity is innate to matter; thus rejecting all the weighty evidence in favor of the dominate concept of matter. Second, most vitalistic proofs are based on the negative rather than the positive side of experimentation. Finally, Haldane says that all vitalisms must contradict the law of the conservation of energy. Again this criticism is directed primarily at Driesch's suggestion that the vital force is non-energetic. Haldane observes that guidance or direction coming from the outside of the material organism implies that energy is being created.

Next Haldane moves to his objections against traditional mechanism. The first objection is parallel to an objection to vitalism; namely, mechanism is willing to make huge assumptions with little real evidence. For example, physics in establishing the laws of nature assumes the fact of cause and effect. Physiology translates the concept of cause and effect into that of stimulus and response. Haldane suggests that there was not enough real evidence to state plainly that physical or chemical cause and effect, and stimulus and response, are the same.3

One reason that the above objection has some
justification is that the same stimulus may cause very
different and unpredictable responses in different
organisms, or even in the same organism. This
clearly violates the usual understanding of cause and
effect. Returning to Driesch's experiments, Haldane
also admits that a usual understanding of mechanism
would not account for some of the results that Driesch
achieved.

Thus in place of either a theory of vitalism, or
a theory of mechanism as pure cause and effect,
Haldane proposes his own theory of organism. He points
out that concepts such as matter, energy, mass and
organism are all theories which attempt to give some
unified conception of reality. In particular
Driesch's concept of organism is a model for relating
matter and energy.

Driesch, however, insisted that the concept of
organism be joined with a concept of a vital force --
entelechy. This entelechy was common to all aspects
of life and matter, but it was not the same as the
matter-energy reality. In other words, while he
insisted that a concept of organism applied to all
reality, certain aspects of the matter-energy reality
were excluded from the vital force. Indeed he went on
to say that the concept of organism could be used as
proof for the vital force. Haldane believed that a
concept such as organism should have been formulated in
order to avoid the idea that life can be described as
so much energy passing through so much matter; but,
organism as a concept is no more than a way of
stating that matter and energy are an indivisible
whole. As a concept it does not point to a vital
force. Haldane's suggestion that the concept of
organism describes the indivisibleness of matter and
energy is an important development toward Process
thought.

As understood by Haldane, the concept of organism

does away with many of the problems of dualism. And
it also suggests a new interpretation of evolution:

> Evolution, therefore, takes on a
> very different significance. In
> tracing life back and back towards
> what appears at first to be the
> inorganic we are not seeking to
> reduce the organic to the inorganic,
> but the inorganic to the organic.4

Haldane also takes very seriously the suggestions
of men like Ward and Hocking who say that individual
is a higher concept than organism. Therefore, after
redefining organism, Haldane goes ahead to say that
'conscious organism' -- person -- is a concept higher
than organism, but not all organisms are conscious.

Haldane prefers the term 'person' to that of
individual. He says that philosophy shows that the
central factor of the universe is a personality which
includes within itself the whole universe. We will
fully discuss the term 'personality' later. At this
point a brief distinction between individuality and
personality in this context will be enough. Individuality is the unique character of an entity which
exists independently of any relationships. Personality is the aspect of an entity which exists because
of relationships. Haldane is suggesting that the
essential principle of reality is relatedness. In
particular reality is a relatedness of matter and
energy.

Matter cannot exist apart from energy, and energy
cannot exist apart from matter. This position disagrees with vitalism because it denies that a vital
force directs matter, while matter in no way determines that force. On the other hand, it denies pure
mechanism, which holds that cause and effect is the
complete description of activity.

From the point of view of spiritual evolutionism
Haldane's position is mechanistic because of its

acceptance of matter as an aspect of the source of
activity. From the point of view of vitalism in
general it is mechanistic, because it assumes that the
ultimate nature of relationships between matter and
energy are predetermined. That is, it assumes that the
factor of universal personality depends upon specific
relationships. These relationships are not as simple
as either pure mechanism or vitalism suppose, but they
can in theory be predicted. Organism is the model to
be used in explicating these relationships.

Process will come to agree with much that
Haldane had to say. His concept of organism will be
accepted as a model for the matter-energy reality.
Process will also accept continuity existing between
matter and energy that excludes the need for any outside force working upon matter. Moreover, Process will
see that Haldane's position removes the dualism that
may seem to exist between matter and mind. In a
conscious entity, the relationships between matter and
energy are described by the concept of personality,
rather than simply organism. A personality is a very
complex form of organism. The details of this complexity Haldane did not profess to understand, and it will
be up to later Process thinkers to supply that detail.

Finally Haldane's position implies a meaning for
the term absolute. The term refers to the universal
principle of personality, which is a unity of specific
relationships -- even though the complexity of these
relationships may not be known or understood. The
apparently independent activities of living organisms
are the result of laws of relationship inherent in the
organisms. (Probably Haldane saw the laws of
relationship ultimately denying the independence of
organisms). In other words, he is adopting a theory
of mechanism which allows that the relationships in
living organisms are more complex than the pure
causal relationships of dead matter.

Process will conclude that Haldane's concept of
organism, while essentially correct, does not
necessarily lead to a mechanistic conclusion. Once

the details of the complexity of organism are more
fully understood, a matter-energy reality need not be
seen as mechanistic.

The importance of neo-mechanism to the future of
Process becomes clearer as we move from the work of
Haldane to a consideration of Bernardino Varisco's
concept of 'Being'. Varisco is his book THE GREAT
PROBLEMS says that neo-vitalism caused him to give up
a purely mechanistic -- positivistic -- view in favor
of a form of neo-mechanism which he calls 'Practical
Philosophy'.5 Initially Varisco's formulation appears
to be metaphysical. Like Bergson he divided the mind
into two categories. In the place of Bergson's term
'intellect' he uses the term 'consciousness', which he
says is composed of fragmentary perspectives. Instead
of 'intuition' he uses the term 'subconsciousness',
whose content is a complex unity similar to Bergson's
'duration.' Also like Bergson, Varisco says that this
unity is a potential of pure activity. Of course
activity is not itself conscious in the sense of a
person or a subject.

As Varisco develops his concepts they are seen to
be quite different from Bergson's. Bergson said that
the mechanistic laws, which described the activity of
matter, are products of the intellect alone. Matter
of itself is entropic. It is mind that supplies
activity; matter is not vitalized by activity.
Varisco, however, believes that 'spontaneous activity'
as he calls it is characteristic of all reality. He
does not accept the dualism between mind and inactive
matter.

Certainly Varisco does not ignore the special
aspects of life. Indeed he often uses life to
illustrate his work. For example, he uses life to
show that activity does demand the reality of diversity. He says that consciousness in life is the
product of activity meeting 'interference'. The fact
of interference demonstrates the reality of diversity.
Interference is essentially an epistemological
concept; therefore, we will delay discussing it until

we take up the topic of Varisco's epistemology.

For Varisco the laws of physics, or as he more often says, the mathematical or logical formulations, are implicit in the very fact of 'Being'.6 Being for Varisco is the unifying characteristic of all reality. What happens intellectually, according to him, is that the logic implicit in Being becomes explicit. The intellect does not, as Bergson suggests, impose a false mathematical structure, but makes explicit an already existing structure. All reality has Being and Being has a logical order. Intellect is, so to speak, the discovery of that order. Here we can see a mechanistic position. Order being innate to matter, the mind merely discovers what is already there; the mind itself adding nothing.

However, this is not an effort to deny true diversity. Varisco insists that the very nature of Being is activity, and activity demands diversity. The necessary diversity results from the fact that Being has divided itself into "centers of spontaneity which operate indeterminately, each for itself -- the many, the monads."7

Physics he says includes unity and diversity in its own formulations:

> In physics, spontaneity only makes
> its value felt in so far as it is
> presupposed by the observable facts
> and their causal connections, never
> explicitly. So also vigorous unity
> does not make its value felt explic-
> itly, but only as presupposed by the
> mathematical laws and, jointly with
> spontaneity, by the causal laws --
> physical in the strict sense. Laws
> and facts given -- physics has need
> of nothing else.8

For Varisco, any observable activity represents a center of spontaneity. The most elementary center of

activity is what he calls an atom. Earlier in this
work we described atomism as one of the mechanistic
theories which vitalists suggested could not be
reconciled with life. Now Varisco is going to show
that this idea about atomism is not necessarily true.

Second, we must observe that from the point of
view of physics the influence of spontaneous centers
within the universe is totally negligible: the
necessity within the universe always being the same.
What makes for evolution in one area will be absolutely balanced by devolution in another part of the
universe. This does not mean that variation is mere
appearance. It does mean that the necessity, which is
the universe, is a constant, and is so measured by
physics. It is an absolute constant.

To the vitalists' position Varisco says that their
theories for the uniqueness of life are unfounded, if
this uniqueness is purported to negate the mathematical
laws. However, Varisco's position also criticizes
physics for its formulation of the theory of entropy.
He argues that the very necessity which makes the
universe Be, excludes the possibility of the universe
tending towards an end. On the other hand, this does
not suggest that our solar system or even life, as we
know it, is permanent. Varisco would say that the
dissolution of one system is merely a condition of
another being formed.

To summarize Varisco's position: Being is a
given. Activity is the essential nature of Being.
This activity manifests itself in spontaneous centers
of Being, because activity consists of unity and
diversity. However, the activity of the universe is
absolute -- a constant. Physics for Varisco was quite
correct in its discovery that reality is mechanistic.
Yet in formulating universal laws it tends to overlook
the fact of centers of spontaneity.

The preceding does not represent a complete answer
to the vitalists' positions on entropy. Their point
against entropy centered on the fact that an organism

appears to represent an increasing manifoldness. This would contradict the history of entropy understood as an increasing disorder. To answer this point, Varisco says that the centers of spontaneity form bodies.

> Every body is a system, bound to-
> gether and constituted by causal
> nexuses, external and internal.
> The difference between organized
> and unorganized bodies must be
> referred to the differences between
> the said causal nexuses.9

In other words, as spontaneous centers are connected causally, the connections produce variations in
activity different from the variations demonstrated by
the original centers. An organism represents this
point. The centers which compose it take on new variations in activity because the activity is now partly
determined by the centers interfering with one another.
Thus an organism is essentially mechanistic. Nevertheless, this mechanism remains quite consistent with
spontaneity.

Like Haldane, Varisco concludes that neither vitalism nor pure mechanism is an adequate formulation of
reality. Vitalism does not account for the continuity
of reality, and mechanism ignores diversity. The
reason is that vitalism in attempting to explain activity without reference to matter ends in dualism. On
the other hand, materialism gives rise to vitalism because it neglects to recognize a clear fact; namely,
that activity is a necessary condition of reality and
that activity demands diversity. The 'Being' of reality is not explained by materialism, but is merely
assumed. Here Varisco agrees with the vitalists.

It is the fact of Being that is the common aspect
of all reality. This is unlike Haldane's principle of
organism in that organism assumes Being, but Being does
not assume organism. Therefore, Being is the more
primordial formulation. Being, says Varisco, is the
uncontested principle of unity in the universe.

If one starts from the principle of Being, unity and diversity may then be explained. The unity has already been explained. The factor of diversity results from Being manifesting itself in centers of activity. These centers are spontaneous in that they interfere with one another in patterns that are not predetermined. That is, no pattern of organization is ultimate. Each organization in one area of the universe is balanced by a decrease in the organization of another area. Varisco does not hold that the particular matter-energy relationships are predetermined. All that is predetermined is that some relationships will occur. The unity of the cosmos depends upon relationships, but any of the relationships which now <u>are</u> could equally well <u>not</u> have been.

To put this last point in another way, no particular organization is permanent.10 The permanence of an organization would imply that the content of Being changes ultimately. This is not the case. Being allows variations within itself, but these variations do not affect the absolute content of Being. The ultimate remains a total unity because changes do not alter it as a unity. In this sense mechanism is right in viewing reality as determined by the principle of unity. And this unity is what physics describes in its absolute cosmic laws.

The problem with Varisco's system is his understanding of the concept Being, which continues to deny ultimate meaningfulness to diversity. Whatever new organizations are achieved, these ultimately make no difference to the cosmos. Haldane and Varisco explain diversity, but they leave the conclusion that diversity has no meaning. Man, on the other hand, seeks both individual meaningfulness and permanence. Meaningless diversity is no better, from the human point of view, than the total denial of diversity. Clearly Varisco agrees that the mechanistic use of the term absolute has no ontological basis, as no abstract physical principle can account for the existence of activity. It is to vitalism's credit that this point was made clear.

On the other hand, contrary to vitalism, both Haldane and Varisco suggest that when rightly interpreted the source of all activity can be seen as innate within matter. In particular what we know as activity results from the irregular distribution of units of energy throughout the universe. Furthermore, energy's distribution can be analyzed according to its organization into matter. In any particular case the thorough understanding of the organization of matter can determine its necessary energy potential, i.e., the necessary nature of its future activity. Yet this fact does not negate the principle of spontaneity resulting from the irregular distribution of matter-energy in the universe. Should one have a cosmic perspective, irregular distribution would in no way change the absolute balance between matter and energy. Thus we are again at the point of stating that for Varisco, and indeed for Haldane, diversity does not finally change the universe as a whole, and thus diversity cannot be said to have ultimate meaning.

1 Haldane, J.S. MECHANISM, LIFE AND PERSONALITY.
     (London: John Murray, 1913). pp. 17-18.
2 ibid. p. 27.   3 pp. 31-32.   4 p. 100.
5 Varisco, Bernardino. THE GREAT PROBLEMS. trans.,
     R.C. Lodge. (London: George Allen, 1914). Intro.
6 ibid. p. 232.   7 p. 139.   8 pp. 243-244.
9 p. 248.   10 p. 267.

54

CHAPTER VII

EMERGENT EVOLUTIONISM

Vitalism's point was not only the reality of diversity, but that diversity was itself meaningful. Neo-mechanism may have allowed for the reality of diversity, but it then struck down any possibility of this diversity being meaningful. Two philosophers attempt to take the best results of vitalism and neo-mechanism and incorporate them into another system. This new system is often called "Emergent Evolutionism". It trys to combine unity and diversity into a principle of activity in such a way that both can be seen as equally meaningful. C. Lloyd Morgan is the name most widely associated with Emergent Evolutionism. The central principles of his thought are found in INSTINCT AND EXPERIENCE published in 1913. However, in the two volumes of his Gifford Lectures published in 1923, under the titles EMERGENT EVOLUTION and LIFE, MIND, AND SPIRIT he expands and clarifies his thinking. In part this clarification is the result of his response to another development of emergence offered by S. Alexander in his work SPACE, TIME AND DEITY. Therefore, it is better to begin with Alexander's work.

The reasoning behind the formulation made by neo-mechanism will be greatly clarified by the work of Samuel Alexander, who, as we will see, shares many formulations with Varisco. Involved for both is the desire to find some factor which absolutely unifies all reality. Otherwise, the argument that there is an ultimate difference between the activity of matter and life cannot be well refuted.

We can say that Varisco's and Alexander's positions generally represent the same basic assumption that activity consitutes all of reality. However, Varisco did not consider the point that bodies, which are complexities of activity, appear to fall into charateristic categories. For example, there are organisms that think, and organisms that do not think. Varisco's system of spontaneous and ultimately impermanent organizations does not explain why many organizations appear to occur in regular and orderly successions. The order of evolution is an example of a pattern which Varisco's system does not explain. Alexander attempts to give a new explanation of the common factor of reality, which will explain why there are categories of bodies similar to one another in the variations that they show, and which will account for why these variations are permanent.

We will begin in Alexander's work with his assumption that change is totally extra-material. Space-Time is for Alexander the necessary component of change, i.e., it is both unity and diversity. Matter is not necessary to activity. Thus we could think of change with or without matter being involved.[1] This sounds very much like a vitalistic position. In fact Alexander says that it is correct to think of reality as composed of events rather than of objects. "Thus Space-Time," says Alexander, "is a system of motions, and we might call Space-Time by the name of Motion were it not that motion is in common speech merely the general name for particular motions, whereas Space easily and Time less easily is readily seen to be a whole of which spaces and times are fragments."[2]

The particular events in Space-Time Alexander calls "point-instants". A given point-instant may be thought of as an event with relative space (small 's') and relative time (small 't'). Thus he would answer Bradley's question of what relates by saying Space-Time. Nevertheless, Space-Time does not exclude the fact of spatiotemporal relationships.

What he calls matter are modes of Space-Time. At no point does any additional factor such as a vital force appear. What we know as categories of reality, for example, are factors in the determinations of the space-times themselves. Thus he says, "For it is clear that Space-Time takes for us the place of what is called the Absolute in idealistic systems."[3] It is the common factor which relates all reality.

56

Given that which relates is Space-Time, and what is being related are spatiotemporal events, we have yet to see why these events follow particular patterns. Alexander says that the patterns, which we observe, are levels of reality. For Alexander there are five levels of reality: Space-Time, the all-inclusive reality, matter, life, mind and God. We can easily see what Alexander means by Space-Time, but we must next see what he means by saying that these other levels are spatiotemporal events.

Alexander believes that at a certain degree of complexity of motions, of spatiotemporal events, what we call 'matter' emerges. Here it is appropriate to point back to Varisco's term nexus, which was described as a complexity of interfaces which produce variations by interference. At this point Varisco may be clearer than Alexander, as Alexander never says much about the internal workings of the various complexities. He instead describes them externally. Of course, he does say that the levels correspond to various configurations of Space-Time, but he describes the results of the configurations rather than the configurations themselves.

As matter emerges from Space-Time at a given level of complexity, so at a still greater level of complexity life emerges from matter, and finally when the complexity is still greater, mind emerges in life. Thus each level is a new order of complexity. What still has not been explained is why or how these levels of complexity become permanent. How does it come about that relations are cumulative? Varisco would deny such a permanence by the argument that a greater organization in one section of the universe always corresponded to devolution in another section of the universe. Alexander's position would suggest that something new is being created in the universe. This new factor is the permanence of levels of reality. Thus the universe appears to be more organized with each level, and this violates the understandings of thermodynamics.

To begin with Alexander says that he does not consider every aspect of a level of reality permanent. Instead, each level is characterized by a special feature. For example, to the special feature demonstrated by life Alexander gives the name 'plasticity'. Likewise, the unique factor of mind he calls 'consciousness'. Beyond mind the next emergent level is God. God for Alexander has the empirical quality of 'deity' in the sense that life has plasticity and mind has consciousness.

Each of these special factors is the element of permanence within the respective level of emergence. For example, once the organization of Space-Time has achieved the level of life, the characteristic of plasticity is a factor which is permanent in spite of the fact that specific entities, having this characteristic, are not themselves permanent.

The factor of permanence is called a 'nisus'. A nisus continually draws Space-Time into configurations which represent the emergent levels. The formation of nisus is a oneway street. A nisus prevents the regression from a given level of complexity, once that level has been achieved. However, it does not prevent the development of still greater complexities, some having their own nisus. According to Alexander, the nisus of the greater complexity will include the nisus of any organization less complex than itself. Nisus is also that which draws lesser levels of complexity into its own higher level. The nisus which at present draws the whole universe to itself is Deity.

Next Alexander says that the nisus of each emergent level is the common factor in which all the entities on that level participate. The exception to this rule is deity, in which only the single entity God participates. This is not suprising, as each level of organization has increasingly fewer members. The Space-Time of the universe is absolute -- a constant. A greater organization does not produce more Space-Time; it merely organizes it into more complex configurations. If this was not the case, Alexander's system would violate the laws of the conservation of energy. Of course, even if this position avoids the violation of conservation, it is hard to see how it could avoid the problem of entropy.

Moreover, Alexander's position describes the levels of reality. It appears that these levels are necessary rather than random. In other words, they are the only levels that could have occurred. The levels are themselves determined by the nature of Space-Time.

At one end of the scheme of emergence is Space-Time itself. At the other end is God. According to Alexander the nisus deity is characterized by an organization which includes all lesser nisus, even consciousness. By being drawn into deity the nisus consciousness does not change in quality, rather it continues to allow changes among the entities on its level as more entities are drawn into the level of consciousness. That is, the entities within the level of consciousness reflect change, while consciousness qua consciousness remains changeless. Thus a given nisus does not prevent change even among the entities on a particular level. Likewise, God, the single entity on the level of deity, reflects the fact of change on that level. In other words, God changes as the entities on all other levels change. Yet deity as a principle of unity, which includes every other nisus, does not change. Change and changelessness both occur on the level of deity; as they do on every other level.

The entities on each level maintain the fact of diversity, while the nisus maintains the principle of unity. Remembering that all of this is a result of the activity innate in Space-Time, we can say on the one hand that a nisus creates diversity, as the nisus draws new entities onto its respective level of emergence. On the other hand, the entities on a given level create their nisus; as the nisus does not exist apart from the entities which compose it.

Alexander's position is mechanistic because he associates Space-Time with the term absolute, and then argues that Space-Time is changeless, and that it determines the levels of reality. It is the nature of Space-Time to allow only certain configurations. The most complex configuration, according to Alexander, is the entity God. Apparently God is, and always will be, the only entity on the level of deity. As deity draws entities from other levels into itself, God becomes more complex. Ultimately it seems that all of the configurations of Space-Time will be included in God.

At any moment in history the existence of God does not prevent true diversity. Nor does Space-Time prevent true diversity. They do not prevent diversity, because change is a part of Space-Time and of God. Here we have a mechanistic system which allows true diversity. This diversity is meaningful because it has the cosmic significance of changing the entire universe. Every change is a change in Space-Time and in God. The nisus deity, like any other nisus, is primordial in that it results from the very nature of Space-Time, but the God that presently exists has emerged as have all other entities. Man can know absolutely the levels of emergence; but the concrete content of each level is changing from time to time.

It also seems that in Alexander we are not only dealing with mechanism, but also with monism. Ultimately all entities will be drawn into the entity God on the level of deity. This will produce a single entity on a single level. Space-Time will have returned to itself. This is to be expected. After all Space-Time is absolute.

The most important feature of Alexander's emergence for the history of Process is the attempt to give diversity cosmic meaningfulness. And this diversity is given meaningfulness up until the point that Space-Time returns into itself.

Of course, individual significance is understood within very narrow limitations. Each entity does

60

contribute to the cosmos in the sense that some entities are needed in order for each level of emergence
to be established. Some material entities are needed,
some living entities are needed, some conscious entities
are needed. Alexander disagrees with Varisco, who
said that what now is could just as well not have been.
Alexander insists that some of each type of entity must
be.

On the other hand, the contribution of any one
entity is ultimately no different from that of any
other entity on the same level. For example, men as
men contribute to consciousness, but the value of all
contributions is finally the same. It makes no
difference to the universe what a man does.

We are now ready to see how Morgan understands
emergence; especially as it relates to the possibility
of meaningful individuality. Both Alexander and
Morgan insist that they are not doing metaphysics.
In this sense they are positivists, who reject true
metaphysical speculations. For Morgan the term metaphysics always implies that something is imposed on
nature ab extra. He goes so far as to suggest that to
be metaphysical is to be vitalistic in one's position.4
In this regard to be a vitalist is to insist that some
extra material force determines material bodies.

Alexander's nisus, Berkeley's eternal spirit,
Kant's transcendental ego, Driesch's entelechy, and
Bergson's elan would all, according to Morgan, fall
into the category of forces which determine the
organism. He says:

> The point of my contention is that
> the progress of inorganic evolution
> is replete with events which are
> unforeseeable on the basis of the
> fullest possible experience prior to
> the actual occurrence of such events.
> All that we can do, in science, is
> to correlate the new with the old.5

Morgan wants to use material-events as the starting point for speculations. To speak of the metaphysical 'source' of activity seems to him quite impossible. For example, he says that he can find no evidence that spatiotemporal events take place apart from material reality.6 This is certainly contrary to Alexander's view of events as being only spatiotemporal.

Morgan is prepared to develop a system of emergence that is grounded fully in the experience of material-events. In particular he says that what is meant by the levels of emergence is the emergence of different kinds of relatedness among material events. The common characteristic of a level of emergence is not, as Alexander suggested, a principle of unity outside of the entities themselves. Unity and diversity are within matter, i.e., material events.

Morgan's levels of emergence are matter, life and mind. To the relatedness of each level he gives a name. For example, the relatedness of mind is called 'projicient reference'. Later we will see that by the term projicient reference Morgan suggests the way in which the mind associates qualities with particular stimuli. Thus, to explain the workings of mind, one need not go beyond material-events within the conscious entity.

The purpose of Alexander's concept of nisus was to account for the relative permanence observed within levels of emergence. The problem for Morgan is to explain the principle of unity between material events. To account for permanence or unity Morgan assumes something which he calls a 'Plan'. On each level of emergence this plan takes a different form. In matter the plan is known as physical laws. In organic life the plan is called heredity. On the conscious level the plan is a scheme of values. The concept of plan does not, however, eliminate individuality. In the case of man, for example, at the base of value or worth there are many conscious minds.

The number of conscious minds does not prevent
unity. The general plan of value provides the needed
unity, because all minds participate within that
same realm of reality.7

A plan is the scheme of a given level of emergence, that has been shaped and created by the
entities which compose it. This implies that the particular levels of emergence are not predetermined, but
are themselves the result of emergence. Diversity and
unity develop at the same time. Unity does not merely
leave room for diversity. Alexander, of course, said
that the levels were predetermined and simply allowed
for individual entities within themselves.

It is Morgan's plan which replaces Alexander's
nisus. The great advantage of Morgan's position is
that a more firm concept of individuality is allowed.
In the case of man, as with other entities, the
specific actions of each individual affect the plan.
Thus for man a concept of value is supposed, as the
actions of individuals have ultimately different
meanings.

Next Morgan must explain how unity and diversity
can develop at the same time. Thus far he has merely
argued that his description is the best possible view
of material evidence. To finally support his formulations Morgan introduces a specific doctrine of God.
He admits that theism is not subject to rigorous
proof. However, he argues that accepting theism makes
his system complete. That is, it makes his system
complete by showing that ultimately both unity and
diversity must emerge alongside one another.

Morgan's doctrine of God's nature must be understood in terms of individuality and personality as
God's two poles. The former pole is the pole of
absolute uniqueness; the latter pole is the pole of the
universal features of the given levels of emergence.
'Bi-polarity' is also what constitutes the 'personal'.

All reality, according to Morgan, follows the

63

bi-polar model. All reality is composed of personality, which is relative, and individuality, which is
absolute. In this way Morgan's bi-polar God is able
to harmonize unity and diversity, as Alexander said
that Space-Time could do. However, Morgan says that
there is a significant difference between his position
and that of Alexander. Alexander is willing to call
Space-Time absolute. Morgan prefers not to call God
absolute, even though God and Space-Time appear to
have the same function. The term absolute when applied
to God is easily interpreted to suggest that God has
no relationships.

In Morgan's system the absolute pole has retained
the function of providing unity. In order to account
for his understanding of emergence Morgan must
qualify the meaning of the term absolute in two very
important ways. First the relative pole has been made
equal to the absolute pole. Second, the absolute pole
and the relative pole are made bi-polar aspects of God.

Through the above formulation Morgan has suggested
a way to overcome one of the greatest problems for
Process thought. As we have said, all Process thinkers
agree that activity can be explained only if there is
true unity and diversity. If unity is absolute, which
we have shown to be a widespread opinion, then Process
is not able to explain why there is activity at all.
Process up to now has no more explained why the cosmos
is not presently in a unified state, than physics has
explained why the cosmos is not in an entropic state --
if entropy is being rightly interpreted. Strictly
speaking, Process has not explained why there is process rather than no process.

It is this problem that Morgan attempted to
solve. His solution is that process in the cosmos
reflects the ultimate nature of God. The absolute
is not something as great as God, but less than God.
Creation is as it is because it reflects the bi-polar
necessity that is the Creator. An absolute, such as
Alexander's Space-Time, cannot be the creator of a
process. Logically Alexander's formulation suggests

64

that the absolute (Space-Time) creates something that is contrary to its own nature.

Morgan does not attempt to work out all of the implications of his position. For example, he does not explain what is the concrete content of the absolute pole, as it is not all of reality. However, his work clearly implies that absoluteness has both a functional and a concrete reference, which must be seen in terms of a bi-polar universe. In this regard, Morgan is our first example of a Process thinker who begins to accept the full implications of the Process position.

William McDougall is a critic of what Morgan is attempting, because he believes that the materialistic nature of emergence continues to be unable to account for the special qualities of life and mind. In his book MODERN MATERIALISM AND EMERGENT EVOLUTION he makes a distinction among vitalists, animists and mechanists. Briefly the distinctions are: (1) Vitalists believe that the living body must be explained in terms of both mechanistic and teleological principles; (2) Animists identify teleology as guidance by a purposeful Spirit; (3) Mechanism rejects all teleology, regardless of its nature.8

Having earlier discussed McDougall's objections to materialism, we can now see his special reasons for calling emergence mechanistic. McDougall's chief explanation is that matter and mind cannot be combined as the emergent evolutionists suppose. He says, "I suggest that it is not valid; that the words are used to denote two types of synthesis that are fundamentally different and distinct; and that by the use of the words 'configuration' (Gestalt) and 'emergence' it is falsely made to seem that creative synthesis (which undeniably occurs in the mental sphere) occurs in the physical.9

He further points out that the emergent evolutionists never really give any examples of instances of emergent qualities in the physical world. Indeed physical reality, as in the case of Morgan's plan of

65

the physical laws, appears toally predictable. The
qualities of individuality and personality, to which
Morgan refers, appear, so far as McDougall is concerned, only on the level of mind. They cannot be
specifically identified on any level of emergence below
mind. In this way McDougall argues that emergence has
not solved the fact that life probably, and mind certainly, is of a totally different order than matter.

In spite of the continued opposition of animists
such as McDougall, emergence has a profound influence
on the development of Process thought. This is
especially true in the Process thought of Teilhard de
Chardin, to whom we will turn next.

1 Alexander, Samuel. SPACE TIME AND DEITY. (London:
      Macmillan, 1920). Vol. I., p. 43.
2 ibid. p. 61.   3 p. 346.
4 Morgan, C. Lloyd. INSTINCT AND EXPERIENCE. (London:
      Methuen, 1913). Second Edition. p. viii.
5 ibid. p. 151
6 Morgan, C. Lloyd. EMERGENT EVOLUTION. (London:
      Williams and Norgate, 1923). p. 24.
7 Morgan, C. Lloyd. LIFE, MIND AND SPIRIT. (London:
      Williams and Norgate, 1923). p. 273.
8 McDougall, William. MODERN MATERIALISM AND EMERGENT
      EVOLUTION. (London: Methuen, 1934). p. 32.
9 ibid. p. 120. McDougall places the origin of
      Emergent Evolutionism or Emergent Vitalism with
      John Stuart Mill's concept of mental-chemistry.

CHAPTER VIII

TEILHARD DE CHARDIN
AS A PROCESS THINKER

Up to this point we have discussed influences which contributed to the development of Process thinking. It would be partly inappropriate to call many of the men that we have studied Process philsophers, as process in a systematic form was not central in their philosophies. Now, we are ready to consider the works of two great philosophers who may rightly be called Process thinkers: Teilhard de Chardin and Alfred North Whitehead. In many ways their works are quite different. Teilhard draws much more heavily upon the concepts introduced by emergence than does Whitehead. As we have been talking about emergence we will begin with Teilhard's works.

The majority of Teilhard's books were published after his death in 1955. However, many of them were written during the same period in which Whitehead produced his major philosophical writings, and both men illustrate some common influences; as well as different influences. Even though Teilhard's works became available much later than Whitehead's, they represent developments in Process thinking that parallel Whitehead's developments. Also because Teilhard's works appeared later, they do not have as important an influence on the number of other Process thinkers. It was in the 1960's before Teilhard could be considered a real force in philosophy. Nevertheless we must see his work reflecting an early period in Process development. Moreover, in seeing how his work agrees with emergence, we can more easily see how Whitehead differs from emergence.

We shall begin by pointing out something in common between Teilhard and Morgan; namely, Teilhard like Morgan regularly insists that he is not doing metaphysics.1 Likewise both have similar reasons for holding this position. Morgan, we may recall, suggests that if one is to remain grounded in experience -- an experience made up of material events -- it is not possible for science to talk about true metaphysics. Teilhard says that he grounds his work in the experience of the phenomenal world, and therefore finds it impossible to explore the essence of being, apart from entities themselves.2 In matters such as these we are not suggesting that Teilhard was directly influenced by Morgan. Rather one can only observe that both of them are responding to the situation that every form of vitalism persists in ending with a dualism between mind and matter.

We do know that both men were influenced by Bergson, and that they see themselves speaking to his results. At one point Teilhard says, "We have had good reason to smile at Bergson's elan vital. But have we not at the same time thrown it overboard too lightly?"3

With emergent evolution in general Teilhard shares a grounding in a desire to reconcile matter and life. With Morgan in particular he shares a grounding in material events, and a belief that pure mechanism does not explain why there is activity rather than no activity. We will illustrate briefly the two former contentions, and give the latter one greater emphasis.

Teilhard shares with the emergent evolutionists the concept of levels within evolution. For example, he speaks of the movement from atom to cell, to the thinking animal.4 Usually Teilhard speaks of the level of life as the 'bioshpere' and the level of consciousness as the 'noosphere'. The level beyond the noosphere is called 'Omega', and we shall discuss Omega shortly.

Life, according to Teilhard, emerges from matter. He says, "If matter is left to itself, in a sufficient mass and for a sufficient length of time, and in suitable conditions of temperature and pressure, it always in the end, through the effect of chance and numbers, becomes vitalized..."5 In other words, he accepts the general point of view, consistent with emergence, that the various levels are the result of an increased complexity of organization. Likewise, for Teilhard, at a certain level of complexity, life becomes conscious.6

To be conscious according to Teilhard is to be reflective. Teilhard believes that the reflective capacity has become man's chief problem. In particular it is reflection that has led man to make a distinction between matter and life.7 This is very similar to Bergson's position that the intellect creates the material laws. Furthermore, characteristic of Bergson, Teilhard says that the greatest dilemma for modern man is the opposite currents of matter and life.8

For Teilhard matter is essentially a multiplicity. Spirit is a unity. Consistent with Process thought, Teilhard holds that activity requires both unity and diversity. However, within the multiplicity which is called matter there is a potency for unity. This 'potency' for unity is not released until the development or emergence of consciousness.9 As Bergson pointed out, matter qua matter appears to be entropic. On the other hand, the idea of spirit being potentially within matter solves for Teilhard the spirit-matter dualism. "If matter and spirit are regarded as synonyms, the former for multiplicity and the latter of unity, then they are not two heterogeneous or antagonistic things, coupled together by accident or force."10 Matter is multiplicity with the potential for unity, and spirit or consciousness is the unity that has been actualized in the material world.

Matter is generally thought of as being unified by virtue of absolute physical laws. Life or spirit, on the other hand, is used to prove the fact of individuality. The usual formulation would be to suggest that life proves individuality. On the contrary, Teilhard sees the spiritual as a unity, a complex organization. The reality of this organization depends upon a previous material multiplicity. He goes so far as to say, "No spirit (not even God within the limits of our experience) exist, nor could structurally exist without an associated multiple..."11

We must understand what Teilhard means by saying
that matter is a multiplicity, and that spirit provides a unity. He says that the first two laws of
thermodynamics are inadequate to explain the present
order of the universe. Taken together they suggest
that greater organization is impossible without an
increase in energy, and that there is no possible
material source of the energy required for organization. Thus matter is inherently disorganized. It is
a multiplicity. Alone material laws cannot explain
unity or organization. Here we are reminded of F.H.
Bradley's arguments that materialism could not account
for what relates.

In order to account for unity Teilhard suggests a
third law, the 'law of organization or reflection of
energy.'12 Keeping in mind the necessity of avoiding
contradiction with the laws of conservation and entropy
Teilhard says, "To think 'the world' (as physics is
beginning to realize) is not merely to register it but
to confer upon it a form of unity it would otherwise
(i.e., without being thought) be without."13 This
unity is spiritual or conscious, and while not separate
from matter, it creates an organization that counters
entropy.

Consciousness represents an organization beyond
entropy. Consciousness through reflection is capable
of intellectually embracing the world.14 The achievement of the level of consciousness, says Teilhard,
must be the basic movement within evolution.

Another name which Teilhard uses for his third
law of the organization of energy is 'involution'. To
illustrate involution he uses the model of 'person'.
His use of person is quite like the use of that term
by Morgan, i.e., to become personal is to find a unity
through individualization. However, Teilhard prefers
to speak of one becoming 'centered' rather than individualized. Thus Teilhard says that the outcome of
involution is the 'Center'. The Center is that which
represents a complex unity of all consciousness.

The one name commonly used for the Center is Omega. "Omega, in the form that the evolutionary structure of the world demands for it, is much more than the 'real' image which is destined to take shape in the future at the focus point of the convergent universe."15

In other words, reflection of energy is the bringing together of all diversity into a complex unity. The new law of energy is manifested within human consciousness, which itself is a unity of a multiplicity of factors. Both the multiplicity and the unity are already present within reality, but they are brought together into a total complex-unity -- a center of consciousness. It is in this third law that we find the answer for why there is organization rather than disorganization. The fact of unity and diversity reflects the nature of the ultimate source of activity, the conscious Center.

As we might expect from Morgan's influence, Teilhard also speaks of the Center or Omega as being personal. The term absolute applies to it in the sense that it ultimately holds all consciousness within itself. Furthermore, Teilhard says that Omega already has a concrete content; the level of consciousness organization already achieved. Teilhard makes Omega bi-polar. One pole or part of Omega he says is transcendent -- independent of evolution. The other aspect has always been emerging.16

Teilhard feels that by its very nature Omega -- God -- has always been able to ultimately unite all diversity. The degree of diversity does not change this ability. Therefore, in terms of the ability to unite God is transcendent. In this respect God determines reality, but it is a determination which does not preclude diversity. God is also immanent, i.e., he participates in relationships. Only within this understanding, according to Teilhard, can one account for conscious activity.

In general Teilhard agrees with Morgan's

71

formulation that activity must have its source in a
bi-polar God. Then Teilhard goes much further than
Morgan in the description of the pole of unity. It is
absolute in the abstract sense that by inner necessity
it is always a principle of unity. It also has a concrete content; namely, it is a unity of all the reality
that has reached the level of consciousness. No true
organization exists outside of the absolute pole, but
disorganized matter, having only the potential for
unity may exist outside of it without contradiction.

We must recall that unity has been defined as an
increase in organization. Organically speaking, organization intensifies individuality and in turn is
developed through this intensification. Thus the
above understanding of the absolute pole can be reached
only in company with the bi-polar concept of the
universe.

So far Teilhard's use of the term absolute is
clearly consistent with the Process understanding of
the role of the absolute outlined in the Introduction.
However, for Teilhard the absolute pole is only one
aspect of God, who is the ultimate source of activity.
Indeed matter, multiplicity, demonstrates no activity
other than organization. Absoluteness in reference to
God, the source of activity, must mean an ultimate
organization of all multiplicity, which in fact
Teilhard sees occurring at Point Omega -- somewhere in
the future. Whenever absoluteness refers directly to
some aspect of the source of activity, the nature of
that source must be realized through activity. Because
within such a formulation consistency is maintained
only when the 'source's' absolute aspect determines
activity in the same sense that mechanism's absolute
physical principle determines activity.

In Teilhard's system true multiplicity is grad-
ually exhausted, as all reality becomes centered. Of
course Teilhard argues that unity has a complex
nature, and thus it does not eliminate diversity.
Nevertheless, it is clear from our study that the disorganized matter outside of consciousness, and the

spiritualized individuals are not the same. Furthermore, in order to include disorganized matter in his system Teilhard has made it an essential factor in activity. How activity can continue after all reality has been spiritualized remains an unanswered question. Indeed, Teilhard offers no arguments that show how Point Omega will be anything less than an entropic state. Depending upon how one looks at matter, the entropic state may be viewed as absolute disorganization or as an absolutely uniform field.

Exactly how Teilhard envisaged the internal structure of the universe at Point Omega is not clear. If at that point true diversity is eliminated, which is a possible conclusion, then one might conclude further that diversity could not be called an ultimate aspect of God's nature; and therefore the source of activity is not finally explained.

However problematic Teilhard's account of activity may be on a metaphysical level, we must remember that he was not doing metaphysics. On the physical level, there is a great deal of important information connected with his description of activity in the phenomenal world. Activity is an organization -- a process -- rather than pure cause and effect. Process for Teilhard is an interplay between unity and diversity. The diversity is supplied by matter and the unity is the result of the complex organization of matter onto the level of consciousness. Mind is a very complex organization of matter. The metaphysical implications of such an idea may not be clear in his works. But, much that Teilhard says will be seen to have great importance as we investigate the position of Alfred North Whitehead.

1 Teilhard de Chardin. THE PHENOMENON OF MAN. trans.,
    Bernard Wall. (London: Collins, 1959). p. 31.
2 ibid. p. 31.

3 Teilhard de Chardin. APPEARANCE OF MAN. (London:
    Collins, 1965). p. 261.
4 Teilhard. PHENOMENON OF MAN. p. 188.
5 Teilhard de Chardin. THE ACTIVATION OF ENERGY.
    trans., Rene Hague. (London: Collins, 1970).
    p. 208.
6 ibid. p. 156.   7 p. 23.
8 Teilhard de Chardin. CHRISTIANITY AND EVOLUTION.
    trans., Rene Hague. (London: Collins, 1971).
    p. 109.
9 ibid. pp. 30-31.
10 Teilhard. ACTIVATION OF ENERGY. p. 124.
11 Teilhard de Chardin. HUMAN ENERGY. trans., J.M.
    Cohen. (London: Collins, 1969). p. 57.
12 Teilhard. ACTIVATION OF ENERGY. pp. 40-41.
13 Teilhard. PHENOMENON OF MAN. p. 274n.
14 Teilhard. ACTIVATION OF ENERGY. pp. 323-324.
15 ibid. p. 112.   16 pp. 112-113.

CHAPTER IX

A.N. WHITEHEAD'S
CONCEPT OF DIPOLARITY

Teilhard was concerned with the dualistic position faced by vitalism. So he adopted an emergent position. However, emergence, as McDougall points out, maybe a form of materialism. Teilhard speaks about the spiritual, but his is a sort of pantheistic spiritualism.

Whitehead is sympathetic to much the emergent evolution has to say. Like the emergent evolutionists in general he beileves that both unity and diversity are inherently within creation.1 But he is also like Alexander in suggesting that 'events' rather than 'objects' constitute the real world.2 For example he says,

> My own view is a belief in the
> relational theory both of space
> and time, and of disbelief in the
> current form of the relational
> theory of space which exhibits
> bits of matter as the relata for
> spatial relations. The true
> relata are events.3

Finally he speaks of the division of nature into appearance and reality as 'bifurcation', rejecting this idea in company with Alexander, Morgan and Teilhard.

Whitehead's conception of emergence is different from those discussed before. His own position is probably most like that of Alexander's. Nevertheless, while like Alexander he has pure events rather than material-events at the basis of reality, he is unlike even Alexander in his understanding of the way in which events relate. For Alexander the events interact with each other; but for Whitehead the events extend over each other, so that every successive event includes all of the events that led up to it. Furthermore, Whitehead does not hold that the events are composed of Space-Time. We will consider what does constitute events in a moment.

It is interesting to note that Morgan in his reading of Whitehead's CONCEPT OF NATURE saw Whitehead suggesting something which is totally opposite to the emergent view. Morgan says, "For Mr. Whitehead, as I gather, mind is an order of being wholly disparate from 'nature'...4 If this point is true, Morgan's view might tend to place Whitehead in the category of animists. Indeed, McDougall, a leading exponent of animism, agreeing in part with Morgan, does not place Whitehead in the class of modern materialists. Rather he says that on many points Whitehead's view is consistent with his own animism.5

In the CONCEPT OF NATURE there is considerable justification for understanding Whithead as seeing mind wholly disparate from nature. For example, he says that objects situated in events are intellectual abstractions.6 That is to say, objects are the result of the mind working on nature -- at least this is a possible interpretation of what Whitehead is saying.

Sections of Whitehead's RELIGION IN THE MAKING tend to confirm what has just been said. He speaks of the physical and the spiritual worlds.7 He says that the concrete fact is always 'dipolar', i.e., having a physical and a mental pole.8 In other parts of the same book he speaks of the world as two sided. One side is matter of fact; the other side is ideals.9 In view of such remarks, it is not difficult to see why some readers of early Whitehead concluded that here was a potential animist, willing to accept something of the dualism that vitalism and animism found almost impossible to escape.

On the other hand, McDougall realized that Whitehead, if he was an animist, was not traditonal in his approach. In particular, McDougall is concerned with Whitehead's decision to use the concept of 'organism'. He says, "And with due deference to those philosophers who like Whitehead tell us that the whole of nature consists of organisms, I venture to question whether the word 'organism' can properly be applied to inorganic things that are not the products of design or of teleological causation."10

McDougall's concern from the animists' viewpoint is understandable. The first philosophy of organism that we considered, that of Hans Driesch, was vitalistic and was so recognized. Next we considered Haldane's theory of organism, which was mechanistic, and which like Whitehead's system proposed to include the inorganic. It is small wonder, therefore, that McDougall was suspicious of the term.

In view of the above, it would be helpful to examine whether Whitehead is an emergent evolutionist, or an animists, or if in fact he is producing something different from either of these positions. The place to begin is a more careful look at Whitehead's use of the concept 'organism'.

The concept of organism as a model for reality arises from the problem that life presents to science.

> The status of life in Nature is the standing problem of philosophy and of science. Indeed, it is the central meeting point of all the strains of systematic thought, humanistic, naturalistic, philosophic.11

The concept of organism for Whitehead begins with the Process emphasis of activity being composed of unity and diversity. The principle of activity is at the basis of all organisms, and a single organism or event is a center of intensity within the field of activity. All single events are organisms, for him, but an organism my also be composed of a society of events. This being the case, it is appropriate to say that more complex organisms emerge out of antecendent states of less complex organisms.12 Thus as reality is made up of events, and events are defined as organic, we can call 'reality' organic.

77

Whitehead suggests that those organisms which contain only a single event are known to us as molecules or electrons. Organisms composed of a society of events are known to us as living, self-conscious beings. There are a great confusion of structures which are not organisms.13 That is, there are groups of single event organisms, which, as groups, do not have a complexity greater than the single events which compose them. While all structures are composed of organisms, not all structures are themselves organisms.

Whitehead noted that the electron is <u>possibly</u> the basic event of pure activity. It provides unity because it is the same within or without a living organism. Outside of the living body, the electron runs blindly. Within the body it runs according to the plan of the body. This plan is the mental state of the body.14.

According to this view, previous philosophers of organism were quite right in saying that activity was ultimately organic. However, they were wrong when they suggested that 'all' structures are organisms. The emergent levels of matter and non-self-conscious life (if life of this sort actually exists) are examples of non-organic structures. The study of matter and life is nothing but the study of the organization of electrons. Physics' claim that matter and life show no essential differences in structure is true. For example, life is not more organized than matter -- it is organized in a different way. As regards the matter vs. life issue, Whitehead is on the side of physics and is against vitalism and emergence.

On the other hand, Whitehead agrees with Morgan and Teilhard that physics does not answer the question of why there is activity at all; and he agrees with vitalism and emergence that mechanism cannot account for mind, i.e., self-conscious organisms. First of all we must remember that, according to Whitehead, each electron is spontaneous in itself. That is, it has no predetermined purpose. The plan of the body is a coordination of these spontaneities. Within the living

78

body the organization of electrons produces purpose, but the living body is spontaneous just as the electron is. Whitehead calls such an organization a 'society', and says that it is personal.15

Here 'personal' is used much the same as in emergent evolutionism. The person is an increased individual made possible through an increased unity. In fact Whitehead at one point defines being alive as: "Whenever there is a region of nature which is itself the primary field of the expressions issuing from each of its parts, that region is alive."16 He also says that in such a case atom and individual would mean much the same; for both have an absolute reality which their components lack.17

We must note that Whitehead is a very careful maintainer of a vague line between life and mind, i.e., self-conscious life. The point at which life arrives at the quality of mind is important for an emergent position. However, Whitehead's system need only recognize the mental factor within some life forms.

Electron events and mind are always two essential elements of activity. Matter is not essential, nor is any other special level of emergence. Nature is pure activity, and life (mind) gives content to that activity. 18 The one cannot exist apart from the other. He says, "The doctrine that I am maintaining is that neither physical nature or life can be understood unless we fuse them together as essential factors in the composition of the 'really real'..."19

Morgan was right in observing that Whitehead made mind primordial. It is not a factor that emerges, but it is an essential aspect of reality. However, Morgan misses the point that Whitehead is not denying the equal reality of the physical, nor does he deny the unity of the two. Furthermore, McDougall is wrong even to consider that Whitehead might be an animist. Whitehead does not say that mind animates nature. Mind for Whitehead is only one of two factors necessary for activity. Likewise, McDougall's comment that Whitehead applies the term organism to inorganic things is a misconception. Whitehead actually says that things which are not themselves organisms are made up of organisms.

We have suggested that electrons are the necessary diversity, and that mind is the necessary unity, which together account for activity. Yet as electrons and self-conscious beings are organisms, electrons must be understood as having unity within themselves, and self-consciousness must be understood to contain diversity. It seems we have not quite clarified the meaning of the 'plan' by which Whitehead says that organisms form organic societies.

The point of positing organic societies is the need to account for permanence. Varisco's spontaneous centers of activity are quite like Whitehead's electrons. However, Varisco had to admit that his centers always came together in a random fashion, and that the resulting patterns had no necessary permanence. Whitehead, on the other hand, does want to allow permanence in terms of organic societies.

In order to do this, Whitehead, like Teilhard and Morgan, must introduce a concept of God. It is God who provides the permanence to unity. Unlike Teilhard and Morgan, Whitehead's position implies two different understandings of unity. The first is a principle of unity which exists within events; and the second is a 'nexus' or unity of an organic society of events. This second understanding of unity is also called the 'mental pole', and it is absolute when understood as the mental pole of God. The mental pole of God is complemented by a physical or relative pole. Thus Whitehead agrees with Teilhard and Morgan that the existence of anything rather than nothing depends upon the fact that God is 'dipolar', and that the term absolute refers to one pole of God.20

Permanence is made possible by the absolute pole, because any unity formed among events is retained in it. Thus in terms of the absolute pole there is an increasing organization. But this organization does not change the fact that events have a unity within themselves that is not destroyed by the organization of the absolute pole. Morgan and Teilhard, on the other hand, suggested that unity depended entirely upon organization. Their formulations meant that entities are ultimately determined by the absolute pole, as the organization of that pole implied a decrease in multiplicity. On the contrary, organization, for Whitehead, intensifies multiplicity. He says that the organization of the absolute pole does not decrease multiplicity. Another way of presenting this point is by saying that God is an event which participates in all organic societies. Thus God is ultimately related. The absolute or mental pole of God becomes a unity of all the relationships in which God participates.

If multiplicity is a given, Whitehead argues, unity must be seen in terms of 'true' multiplicity; otherwise one ends up by suggesting that what emerged is different from what is given, i.e., the 'given' multiplicity emerges into unity. The contradictory nature of such a formulation Whitehead calls the 'ontological principle.' 21 In other words, any organization must have continuity with less organized states.22 This continuity is what emergence did not show. Its formulations suggest that process eliminates diversity. The elimination of diversity can hardly be seen as implicit in the fact of diversity as a given. Thus for Whitehead a 'plan' allows for permanence, without determining the cosmos or eliminating the individuality of entities.

In the following quotation concerning human social structure Whitehead illustrates his point that organization intensifies rather than reduces individuality;

> Indeed, one general end is that these
> variously coordinated groups should
> contribute to the complex pattern of
> community life, each in virtue of its
> own peculiarity. In this way

81

individuality gains the effect-
iveness which issues from
coordination, and the freedom
obtains power necessary for its
perfection.23

In summary, Whitehead's point is that the principle of unity is not limited to the absolute pole of
God. The principle of unity is one aspect of the
process in which all entities, including God, participate.   'Creativity' is the name that Whitehead
gives to the ultimate principle of process. The
principle of creativity will be discussed in Chapters
XIX and XX. At the moment, we are only interested
that the term absolute is not applied to the principle
of creativity.

In its abstract aspect the absolute pole is a
unity or organization of all relationships brought
about by God, as an actual entity, participating in
each relationship. The concrete content of the
absolute pole is the unity of all those relationships
that have led to the present level of organization.
Outside of the unity of all past relationships, which
is the absolute pole of God, exists the multiplicity
of entities, each having independent unity in terms of
its own present. In one aspect all entities have an
inner necessity by which they are the same from
instant to instant. Within a dipolar context this
unity does not prevent entities relating.

Every entity has an abstract aspect, but this
aspect is absolute only in the entity God; for only in
God is the conrete content of the absolute pole made
up of all past relationships. Not only is the
absolute pole less than God, but it is also less than
the ultimate principle of unity. The ultimate
principle of unity , which is an aspect of creativity,
has no concrete content. One has no reason to suggest
that in order for the term absolute to be applied to
one aspect of God that aspect must have as its
concrete content all of reality. The Whiteheadian
universe is not heading toward an ultimate concrete

82

unity. If the latter were the case, then the use of
the term absolute by Whitehead would have deterministic
implications. One factor unique to Whiteheadian
Process thought is its success in eliminating all
determinism. Nevertheless Whitehead wants to retain a
reference for the term absolute, because no other term
can replace it.

Whitehead's thought is consistent with mechanism
in two respects. First it agrees that cosmic activity
is innate within reality. Second, it agrees that a
continuity exists within what we call matter, life,
and mind. For Whitehead this continuity is an organic
continuum characterized by atomic structure. In other
words, all reality can be analyzed as built up from
atomic units.

The second point disagrees with a vitalism which
argues for the total uniqueness of life's activity, or
for a dualism between matter and life (mind). On the
other hand, Whitehead agrees with vitalists that life
demonstrates that the source of activity is not
explained by mechanism's abstract physical principle.

Whitehead concludes with Morgan and Teilhard that
the existence of activity along with permanence depends
upon a God whose dipolar nature is characteristic of
reality. All three agree that one pole of God is
absolute and the other relative. Morgan and Teilhard
differ from Whitehead by being unable to understand
reality as ultimately maintaining God's primordial
nature. That is, the two emergent thinkers seem to
suggest that multiplicity within reality becomes
more and more organized until a single complex unity
is achieved.

Whitehead suggests that organization eternally
intensifies diversity. This is possible because
electrons are themselves composed of unity and
diversity, i.e., activity, even though they represent
single events. The idea that single events are organic
is new. Physics would have said that electrons may
be the simplest units of energy, but it also assumed

electrons without accounting for the cause of their organization. Emergence, and other philosophies of organism assumed that an organism must always be a unity of simple objects or events. Thus most organic theories see unity emerging out of a primordial multiplicity. Whitehead argues that this is a clear violation of the ontological principle. Such a positon means that what emerged was different from what was given. Furthermore, the emergent view leads to determinism, because unity must be something imposed upon the given diversity.

Given his organic view of single events, Whitehead says that they can form organic societies. These organic societies become self-conscious, because a society intensifies the organic nature, i.e., unity and diversity, of the events composing it.

Whitehead's formulations do not deny the law of the conservation of energy. He is not proposing that the organization into a society requires a new form of energy, e.g., elan or entelechy. The society is made up only of the elements which compose it. His system does, of course, refute the present interpretation of entropy; but as we have already pointed out, the concept of entropy says nothing about the source of activity.

In many ways Whitehead's formulations agree with Varisco's point that the activity of the universe divides itself into spontaneous centers. As the centers are spontaneous Varisco saw no way to account for permanence. It is the absolute pole of God that Whitehead uses to solve this problem.

The term absolute in Whitehead's works refers to the pole of unity or the mental pole of God. God's mental pole is a unity of all organic relatedness. The mental pole of God is complete within itself as is a single event or entity. However, God is an entity which participates in all organic societies, and in that regard his mental pole has two additional functions for societies. First, it assures the permanence of the societies by retaining the organization achieved. Second, it is the source of energy for the organization of the society.

In Teilhard's system, for example, the organization of events appeared to be created by the individual events giving up their 'true' individuality in order to create a unity. Thus the individual was subordinated to the unity. Whitehead says that because God is an entity which is a member of all societies, his absolute pole allows for organic-social-unity without the necessity of events giving up their individuality.

We have not shown how Whitehead justifies the conclusion that God is an entity who participates in all relationships. Such a discussion must wait until Chapter XIX, when we take up the issue of creativity. The point here is that the absolute pole provides for the organic-social-unities which we call self-conscious organisms. It does not, as Teilhard and Morgan imply, account for all unity. In Whiteheadian thought unity is present as a factor in single events quite apart from God's absolute pole. In his system diversity always exists along with unity -- process is infinite.

We now see how Whiteheadian thought fits into the context of scientific issues which influenced the rise of Process. There are other influences upon the development of Process that we have not yet considered. These influences are of a more purely philosophical nature. In order to complete the picture of the history of Process we must retrace our steps in order to pick up some additional strands of influence.

1 Whitehead, Alfred North. THE CONCEPT OF NATURE. (Cambridge: University Press, 1920). pp. 12-13.
2 ibid. pp. 14-15.   3 p. 24.
4 Morgan. EMERGENT EVOLUTION. p. 236.

5 McDougall. MODERN MATERIALISM. pp. 111f.
6 Whitehead. CONCEPT OF NATURE. p. 125.
7 Whitehead, Alfred North. RELIGION IN THE MAKING.
   (Cambridge: University Press, 1926). pp.102-103.
8 ibid. p. 118   9 p. 99.
10 McDougall. MODERN MATERIALISM. p. 130.
11 Whitehead, Alfred North. NATURE AND LIFE.
   (Cambridge: University Press, 1934). p. 53;
   and MODES OF THOUGHT. (Cambridge: University
   Press, 1938). p. 202.
12 Whitehead, Alfred North. SCIENCE AND THE MODERN
   WORLD. (Cambridge: University Press, 1925).
   p. 152.
13 ibid. p. 156.   14 p. 111.
15 Whitehead, Alfred North. ADVENTURES OF IDEAS.
   (Cambridge: University Press, 1933). p. 267.
16 Whitehead. MODES OF THOUGHT. p. 31.
17 Whitehead. ADVENTURES OF IDEAS. p. 227.
18 Whitehead. MODES OF THOUGHT. pp. 228-229.
19 Whitehead. NATURE AND LIFE. p. 57.
20 Whitehead, Alfred North. PROCESS AND REALITY.
   (Cambridge: The University Press, 1929). p. 42.
21 ibid. p. 55.
22 Whitehead. ADVENTURES OF IDEAS. p. 238.
23 ibid. p. 86.

CHAPTER X

PHILOSOPHICAL INFLUENCES
ON PROCESS

Scientific mechanism held that a clear distinction could be made between conclusions reached upon experimentation and those upon philosophical speculations. Consistency with the absolute physical laws was the boundary beyond which knowable 'facts' became speculations. From the viewpoint of materialism, philosophy, especially metaphysics, was not useful in uncovering truth.

Beginning with the rise of neo-vitalism some scientists and philosophers became convienced that the physical laws could not account for documented 'facts' about life in general and self-conscious life, i.e., mind, in particular. In the foregoing Chapters we looked at the evidence that supported this conclusion. Of course many of the earlier neo-vitalistic formulations were rejected by later Process thinkers. Nevertheless, other vitalistic conclusions contributed to a radical re-thinking of cosmology, that culminated in such things as Whitehead's development of the concept of a dipolar universe.

The way in which vitalistic and emergent theories came to influence Process thought was in part determined by certain epistemological formulations introduced during the same period. As a preliminary definition we will say that 'knowing' is one activity of 'mind', and that epistemology is the study of that 'activity'. Mechanism argued that the study of mental activity was a specialized form of the analysis of the activity of material particles; as all activity was absolutely determined by physical laws. Of course, if the physical laws are not absolute, then mental activity may not be subject to simple physical analysis. Indeed, Bergson, Ward, Teilhard and Whitehead, among others, suggested that it was mental activity that served as a model for all other activity; rather

87

than that mental activity could be analyzed by mechanistic formulations. The reason for the emphasis on mind was that conscious mental activity alone appeared to illustrate true unity and true diversity. Furthermore, it was possible to develop a metaphysics using conscious mental activity as a model for cosmic activity.

There are many types of conscious mental activity, e.g., remembering, dreaming, learning, thinking, etc. All of these activities produce 'knowable' data; but the data are clearly of different types. Therefore, a problem arises as to how to evaluate mental data. The solution demands a theory of knowing -- an epistemology of some sort. It is at the point of establishing a basis for the evaluation of mental data that an understanding of epistemology became central for Process thought. In the following few Chapters we will be concerned to see how and where Process got its own epistemology.

Process is faced with an initial epistemological problem. Unless activity is chaotic, there must be some principle whereby activity is organized. If the principle of organization is absolute, as in the view of mechanism, then activity is determined by that absolute physical principle. Likewise, if mental activity is seen as ordered, there must be some principle which accounts for this organization. If the principle of mental organization is absolute, then knowing is predetermined. Determinism is one of the very things which Process argues cannot accompany activity. The Process move to a model of the mind as an analogy for activity was an attempt to deny determinism. Unfortunately, demonstrating that physical laws do not explain mental activity is not the same as proving that mental activity escapes determinism.

The point that knowledge of reality must be understood in terms of how the mind functions was a firmly established concept throughout the period of modern mechanism's development. Idealism, for example, had long held that knowledge of material order exists

because mind exists. To assume the material order
would be unchanged in the absence of mind -- materialism's view -- cannot be supported by vitalism.

Whitehead indicated that philosophy's emphasis
upon mind had been a key factor in the separation of
philosophy from science. He says,

> The three centuries, which from the
> epoch of modern science, have revolved
> round the ideas of God, mind, matter,
> and also of space and time in their
> characteristics of expressing simple
> location for matter. Philosophy has
> on the whole emphasized mind, and thus
> has been out of touch with science
> during the latter two centuries. But
> it is creeping back into its old-
> importance owing to the rise of
> psychology and its alliance with
> physiology.1

Until the rise of psychology and physiology, the
procedures for the study of the mind had not been
formulated in a way that the experimantal sciences
could accept as valid research methods. Of course, it
is not unheard of for philosophers to have arrived at
valid conclusions long before the techniques were
available to demonstrate their validity. For example,
atomic theories existed long before the empirical
evidence for atoms. Likewise, as the study of mind
began its modern development, certain previous philosophical speculations began to find new supporters;
sometimes among scientists.

As we have already seen the development of Process
was closely allied with that of modern science. The
connections which the new sciences established between
the modern study of the mind and philosophical speculations on epistemology were of great interest to
Process thinkers. In this regard, one tendency among
early Process thinkers, that becomes obvious almost
at once, is the attempt to take some traditional

epistemologies and use modern data about the mind to
support them.

As Process thinking develops the above procedure
becomes less and less workable. While it is true that
Process found traditional epistemological formulations
useful, one serious problem for Process was the use
that most traditional epistemologies made of the concept absolute.

The decision by Process that true unity and true
diversity are essential to activity, which cannot
occur in a deterministic system, underlies the response
made by Process to epistemological systems. In particular, how the term absolute is used by various systems is critical to Process finding them acceptable.
The understanding of the absolute in mechanism was not
acceptable to Process, but the rejection of this understanding did not immediately suggest an alternative.
Therefore, in Chapters XI through XIX we will see how
the Process understanding of absoluteness developed
not only in response to science but also in response
to philosophical -- especially epistemological --
formulations.

At the beginning of the development of modern
Process thought, Idealism was the dominate philoso-
phical alternative to a materialistic position. R.B.
Perry describes the situation.

> Positivism is philosophy driven into
> the camp of science by loyalty to the
> standards of exact research; romanticism
> is philosophy merged into religion
> through its interest in the same ultimate
> questions. These two tendencies deter-
> mined the course of philosophy in the
> nineteenth century; and they are repre-
> sented today by naturalism and
> idealism respectively.2

It is not difficult to see that a renewed emphasis
on mind encouraged a re-examination of idealism.

John Watson gives a helpful insight into late nineteenth century idealism when he remarks:

> I presume it will be admitted that
> the originator of the philosophical
> doctrine of Idealism was Plato, and
> that Plato conceived of the first
> principle of all things as reason;
> also maintaining that it is in virtue
> of reason, as distinguished from
> sensible perception, that man obtains
> knowledge of that principle. Now
> modern Idealism, as I understand it,
> agrees with Plato on these two points,
> and therefore its claim to the name
> does not seem either arrogant or
> unreasonable.3

In Watson's day there were two primary forms of
idealism: Subjective and Objective. Subjective
idealism is represented by positions such as Berkeley's
in which being depends upon individual consciousness.
The classic problem for this form of idealism is
accounting for how one mind is able to know another.
Objective idealism, on the other hand, is represented
by Hegel and F.H. Bradley. "The central conception of
objective idealism, in other words, is the conception
of a super-personal, or impersonal logical consciousness."4 This form of idealism certainly solves the
problem of the unity of consciousness, but it leaves
one with the dilemma of how to account for true
diversity.

Part of the purpose of the following Chapters is
to explain why the above forms of idealism could not
satisfy Process. The difficulty of reconciling the
Process assumption of the necessity of true unity and
true diversity for the existence of activity with
idealism, suggested that an alternative to idealistic
epistemology was needed. As we will see, certain
Process thinkers began to investigate the possibilities
of adopting some form of "Realism'. In essence
traditional realism was the position that there are

universals within nature, which are not different from perceptions.

Realism might be a complement to objective idealism. If the mind is the seat of unity and organization, as objective idealism suggests, perhaps the diversity required for activity exists outside of the mind in nature. Unfortunately traditional realism had not been formulated to complement idealism, but to refute it. In this refutation, as we will see, it ended by establishing diversity at the cost of unity.

The point to be made here is that, in dealing with the issue of mind, Process sought an epistemology that allowed for both unity and diversity as complementary aspects of conscious mental activity. At this point there would be justification for the assumption that in establishing its definition of activity Process assumed an epistemology. This is true. However, it was through working with the date coming out of science that the importance of the mind, and in turn epistemology, became clear. Therefore, in considering the development of Process one is better off to begin with scientific issues.

In this Chapter we have implicitly suggested two requirements that an epistemology must meet, in order to satisfy the metaphysical formulations that come out in the development of Process. First there must be a principle of limitation which provides a standard for the evaluation of mental data. Second mental activity must be seen as composed of both unity and diversity.

Before looking at the positions of various thinkers, it will be helpful if we establish a provisional connection between the two requirements suggested above. Mechanism, for example, says that knowledge is limited to our understanding the structure and organization of the absolute physical laws. Idealism has another principle of limitation. Perry describes this principle by saying, "Idealism is a form of spiritualism in which man, the finite individual, is regarded as a microcosmic representation of God, the Absolute Individual."5

In either case, the concept of absolute refers to the factor which determines the organization of activity. A correct understanding of the organization of activity must be consistent with the predetermined nature of activity. In the foregoing Chapters we suggested that the term absolute, used in the wider sense, referred to either an abstract physical principle, or to a 'Given' -- the content of which was a unity of all reality. Several times we have pointed out that a concept of unity, whether physical or spiritual, may suggest a static condition within the universe. Both physics' understanding of entropy and spiritualism's concept of a 'final' unity were implicit assumptions that an absolute state was devoid of activity. Nevertheless, both materialism and spiritualism assumed that at present activity occurs.

From a Process viewpoint, the traditional understandings of the wider meaning of the term absolute are inconsistent with activity. However, if one does not see the metaphysical problem, then the term absolute used in either sense implies a limitation imposed upon activity and not a denial of activity. Absolutely free activity is chaotic. In order for there to be any organization within activity, whether it be the organization of physical activity into Laws, or of mental activity into Ideals, the freedom of activity must have limits. Further, it is not hard to see that unity, in the sense of wholeness, and limitation are associated concepts. 'Limited', as used here, describes the present dynamic condition of the universe for a system whose use of the term absolute suggests ultimate determinism.6

Just as Process accepts unity, it also, as we will see, accepts a principle of limitation. That is, it accepts a present dynamic condition of the universe that is not chaotic. However, as Process found it necessary to gain a new understanding of absoluteness, in order to allow for both unity and diversity, so the

93

concept of limitation had to be evaluated by some new standards.

Remembering that this discussion is provisional, we will conclude by drawing a connection between the concept of limitation and epistemology. Limitation is the category through which the quality of unity, i.e., totality, is known to the conscious mind. While materialism held the physical laws to be absolute, and spiritualism made an ultimate unity absolute, knowledge of the precise nature of the physical laws or of the absolute unity was not available at any present instant. What could be known were references to absoluteness in terms of limitations. This point is best made in the discussions that follow.

1 Whitehead. SCIENCE AND THE MODERN WORLD. p. 277.
2 Perry, Ralph Barton. PRESENT PHILOSOPHICAL
    TENDENCIES. (New York: Longmans, Green, 1912).
    p. 38.
3 Watson, John. CHRISTIANITY AND IDEALISM. (Glasgow:
    James MacLehose, 1897). p. xxiii.
4 Perry. PRESENT PHILOSOPHICAL TENDENCIES. p. 135.
5 ibid. p. 113.
6 KANT'S CRITIQUE OF PURE REASON. p. 116.

CHAPTER XI

F.H. BRADLEY'S
OBJECTIVE IDEALISM

In an attempt to discover the developments in epistemology which contributed to Process thought, we will begin with the Objective Idealism of F.H. Bradley. Objective Idealism is ultimately spiritualistic rather than materialistic. That Bradley holds this position is made clear in the following:

> Both nature and my body exist necessarily with and for one another. And both, on examination, turn out to be nothing apart from their relation. We find in each no essence which is not infected by appearance to the other.
>   And with this we are brought to an unavoidable result. The physical world is an appearance; it is phenomenal throughout. It is the relation of two unknowns, which, because they are unknown, we cannot have any right to regard as really two, or as related at all.1

In keeping with a spiritualistic conception Bradley uses the term absolute to refer to a concrete unity of all reality.

> For me the Absolute is there to see that nothing in the world is lost. That effort which for our vision is wasted, passes over beyond our vision into reality and is crowned with success. Of all foolish criticisms (and they are many) which have been directed at the Absolute, the most foolish of all perhaps is that it is useless. And this does not mean that, whatever I do, it is all one to the

Absolute. The Absolute is there
to secure that everywhere the highest
counts most and the lowest counts
least. For it is at once the active
criterion and the supreme power.2

We introduced the above quotation not only to
demonstrate Bradley's use of the term absolute, but
also to pick up the point that he refers to the
Absolute as "the active criterion and the supreme
power." In particular the Absolute is the active
criterion and the supreme power of conscious activity:
sentient experience. Bradley says,

Our conclusion so far, will be this,
that the Absolute is one system, and
that its contents are nothing but
sentient experience. It will hence
be a single and all-inclusive experience, which embraces every partial
diversity in concord.3

One of the Process requirements for an epistemology, as we have said, is that unity must serve as
a principle of limitation for the evaluation of conscious mental activity. In other words, mental
activity would be chaotic if it was not channeled into
unities of experience. Bradley agrees that unity must
serve as a principle of limitation. Next we must see
if Bradley attempts to meet the second requirement of
a Process epistemology, by understanding conscious
activity to be composed of true unity and true diversity. That he has some concept of activity has been
suggested through his reference to the Absolute as the
"active criterion and supreme power."

Both by explicit testimony and also by implicit
structural similarities, Bradley demonstrates that
Hegel influenced his own position.4 What we will
consider in the following pages is that Bradley
adopts something like a Hegelian view about consciousness as being composed of unity and diversity. However
Bradley sees that there are problems in establishing

tne precise significance of the diversity which objective idealism discusses. While Bradley rejects any
alternative to idealism, his awareness of its weakness
has two important results for our study. First,
Bradley's view functions as an example of why objective
idealism cannot serve Process as an epistemology. This
point is important, because objective idealism comes
very close to agreeing with Process. Second, the
rather subtle weakness, which Bradley uncovers, helps
to pin-point idealism's understanding of the Absolute
as the reason for it being finally unacceptable to
Process. Let us being by briefly looking at Hegel's
influence on Bradley.

It is generally agreed that one of Hegel's contributions to philosophy was his 'dialectic'. With regard
to Bradley's work we are especially interested that the
dialectic occurs between unity and diversity, and it is
also what Hegel calls 'Force'.5 Hegal calls force the
essential law of reality. For him force is not a
physical principle, rather it is the organization of
Geist, i.e., mind or spirit.6 Finally, and of special
interest to us is the fact that spiritual reality for
Hegel is consciousness.7 This consciousness Hegel
clearly suggests is composed of unity and diversity.8
However, the diversity in conscious activity is not
that of a number of independent 'consciousnesses'
united by some further principle. Instead Hegel understands that a single universal consciousness divides
itself. "God is Himself consciousness, He distinguishes Himself from Himself within Himself, and as
consciousness He gives Himself as object for what we
call the side of consciousness."9

In spite of his belief in a single consciousness,
Hegel holds that the principle of 'Freedom' allows for
'self-conscious' awareness of individual units called
minds. Of freedom Hegel says, "Freedom considered
abstractly means that the mind is related to something
objective which is not regarded as foreign to its
nature, its essential character is the same as that of
truth, only that in the case of freedom the negation
of the difference of Otherness has been done away with

and absorbed in something higher, and thus it appears in the form of Reconciliation."10   And in explaining the concept of reconciliation he says, "All that we mean by reconciliation, truth, freedom, represents a universal process, and cannot therefore be expressed in a single proposition without becoming onesided."11

For Hegel, the content of self-consciousness is nothing other than consciousness itself. The process of unity becoming diversity and diversity returning itself to unity is the twofold form of Force and the two-sided proposition of universal process.

In returning to Bradley's work we may quickly establish three very important similarities between his formulations and those of Hegel. First, reality for Bradley is dynamic rather than static. It is active -- made up of events.12 Second, active reality must, according to Bradley, be made up of unity and diversity. "We have to take reality as many, and to take it as one, and to avoid contradiction."13 Third, consciousness must be made up of unity and diversity, as it is reality. "Being and reality are, in brief, one thing with sentience, they can neither be opposed to, nor even in the end, distinguished from it."14

Indeed, Bradley's writings go on to suggest that, along with Hegel, he accepts that God (Bradley would also use the term Absolute) divides itself to produce diversity.15 And, like Hegel, Bradley understands that diversity is absorbed back into unity. However, Bradley says that during the dialectical process of universal activity individual conscious minds are a more decisive diversity than Hegel's formulation appears to allow. He says,

> The plurality of presentations is a
> fact, and it, therefore, makes a
> difference to our Absolute. It exists
> in, and it, therefore, must qualify
> the whole. And the universe is richer,
> we may be sure, for all dividedness
> and variety. 16

His particular point is that no explanation is available for the positive 'gain' made in the universe because of the dialectical process taking place. The division of the unity into diversity appears pointless unless this somehow enriches the universe. For the unity to divide itself, and return to itself, does not suggest how the overall process has achieved anything. While Bradley believes that a rational understanding of the universe must be formulated in terms of such a process, he still is concerned because this formulation keeps man ignorant of any final gain. In other words, the individual mind appears to discover that the principle of individuality has value, and it seems wrong to assume that this value is lost in the fact that minds share an underlying consciousness.

There is, of course, the option of suggesting that what seems to be the case does in fact occur; namely, that the process of individual events of knowing somehow qualifies consciousness as a whole. However, the understanding of the term absolute, as referring to a unity of all reality, prohibits this conclusion in Bradley's mind.17

His decision to modify Hegelian idealism grows out of an effort to meet the problem of diversity. In particular he suggests that while rational formulations of reality demonstrate a diversity which cannot be joined with a unity of consciousness, knowledge of the human experience of 'feeling' comes far closer to establishing that the dialectical truth of reality is one with knowledge.

At first the adoption of a model of experience may appear to be a move away from idealism's traditional position; Perry points out that this is not so.

> Reality is defined in terms of an
> absolute congnitive consciousness,
> that is both prior to things known
> in the idealistic sense, and also
> a maximum or ideal, in the absolu-
> tist sense. The Absolute Good of

Plato, and the Infinite Substance
of Spinoza, are thus replaced by
the 'Absolute Ideal' of Hegel...18

The special characteristic of feeling, according
to Bradley, is that it is a complex-unity.19 There is
nothing that is of any significance to life that is
outside of feeling. Feeling is experienced as a whole,
and it is also experienced in any number of distinctions. While it is true that one has not experienced
all of the distinctions possible within feeling, there
is never anything outside of the experience of feeling
in general. To experience all of reality is to feel.

Knowledge, which is the truth about reality, is
reached through feelings. What we know are feelings
about objects, rather than the objects themselves.
This, as Perry pointed out, is not in principle other
than saying that ideas are the content of knowledge.

The unity of feeling, for Bradley, continues to
be the absolute whole of reality. Thus he does not
demonstrate a new usage of the term absolute. However,
he sees a problem involved with the concept of absoluteness. And he introduces feelings to try and correct that problem.

Bradley's work shows that in principle objective
idealism is sympathetic to the Process requirements
for an epistemology. Indeed, it is fair to say that
Bradley's obvious tendencies toward Process may, in
part, account for his use of idealism. Of course,
Bradley seems more aware of the full implications of
the concept that unity and diversity must be a part
of activity, than Hegel did. Modern science can be
thanked for that. Bradley even admits that Hegel's
concept of absoluteness is hard to reconcile with true
diversity. Finally, his efforts to solve this
problem give direction to other Process thinkers.

1 Bradley. APPEARANCE AND REALITY. p. 265
2 Bradley. ESSAYS ON TRUTH AND REALITY. p. 348.
3 Bradley. APPEARANCE AND REALITY. pp. 146-147.
4 ibid. p. 552.
5 Hegel, G.W.F. THE PHENOMENOLOGY OF MIND. trans.,
        J.B. Baillie. (London: Swan Sonnenschein, 1910).
        Vol. I, p. 128.
6 ibid. Vol. II, p. 436.   7 p. 494.
8 ibid. Vol. I, p. 224.
9 Hegel, G.W.F. LECTURES ON THE PHILOSOPHY OF
        RELIGION. trans., E.B. Speirs and J. Burdon
             Sanderson. (London:Kegan, Paul, Trench,
             Trubner, 1895). Vol. II, p. 329.
10 ibid. p. 316   11 p. 347.
12 Bradley. ESSAYS ON TRUTH AND REALITY. p. 30.
13 Bradley. APPEARANCE AND REALITY. p. 33.
14 ibid. p. 146   15 p. 527.
16 p. 226.   17 p. 446.
18 Perry. PRESENT PHILOSOPHICAL TENDENCIES. p. 175.
19 Bradley. ESSAYS ON TRUTH AND REALITY. p. 174.

CHAPTER XII

NEO-VITALISM'S EPISTEMOLOGY

Certain discoveries in biology, most of which were discussed in our earlier Chapter, led men such as Bergson and Driesch to conclude that mechanism's concept of physical laws was inadequate to account for life's activity. Because of this, they found themselves rejecting physical activity in favor of some alternative metaphysical source of activity. Thus they held that the activity of life, especially self-conscious life, was not limited by the structure of matter, and that conscious activity required both unity and diversity, supplied by some vital force.

From the viewpoint of epistemology the problem for vitalism is to establish some principle of limitation, which will keep conscious activity from being seen as chaotic, and at the same time allow for diversity. On the issue of limitation objective idealism and mechanism were really quite similar. Both held that activity, whether spiritual or physical, was determined. As we saw in Bradley's presentation, the ultimate determination of activity is a problem to the significance of diversity.

To avoid determinism and establish true diversity Bergson not only rejected the absoluteness of physical laws, but also adopted an 'intuitional' epistemology, that had elements contradictory to idealism's position. Likewise, Driesch, seeing that a principle of limitation is necessary for conscious activity, but wishing to avoid determinism, also developed new insights about the theory of knowing.

Bergson holds that intuition, rather than intellect, is the more important aspect of consciousness. According to Bergson, rational analysis, divided reality into a series of unrelated points.

> In short, the world the mathematician deals with is a world that

> dies and is reborn at every instant --
> the world which Descartes was thinking
> of when he speaks of continued creation.
> But in time thus conceived, how could
> evolution, which is the very essence of
> life, ever take place? Evolution im-
> plies a real persistence of the past in
> the present, a duration which is, as it
> were, a hyphen, a connecting link.1

Bergson regularly uses biocentric illustrations of individual consciousness functioning as intuition. Some of his clearest examples center around a discussion of the intensity of a feeling. He says, "To say love, hatred, desire, increase in violence is to assert that they are projected outwards, that they radiate to the surface, that peripheral sensations are substituted for inner states: but superficial or deep-seated, violent or reflective, the intensity of these feelings always consists in the multiplicity of simple states which consciousness dimly discerns in them."2

In other words, Bergson is suggesting how feeling illustrates that the intuitive or durational aspect of consciousness is additive. Intensity, for example, is a new factor created by the addition of sensation to sensation. The addition does not result in a series of isolated feelings -- intensity is a single feeling. "Continuity of change, preservation of the past in the present, real duration -- the living being seems, then, to share three attributes with consciousness."3

Furthermore, the addition, illustrated by inten- sity, could not have been predetermined. The particular unity produced could only have come about when it happened. Otherwise one would be forced to suggest that the feeling existed before it was felt, and that says Bergson is impossible. This point is expanded in the following:

> Let us seek, in the depths of
> experience, the point where we feel
> ourselves most intimately within

> our own life. It is into pure
> duration that we plunge back, a
> duration in which the past, always
> moving on, is swelling unceasingly
> with a present that is absolutely
> new.4

The unity of the past serves as a limitation of
present conscious activity, without absolutely determining that activity. New events are included in the
durational past, which nevertheless retains the inner
necessity of being a present unity of all that is past.
Both because of its inner necessity, and because it
serves as a principle of limitation for conscious
activity, the term absolute may be applied to duration.
Used in this reference the term absolute does not preclude diversity.

For Bergson the concept of absoluteness is
retained as being necessary to account for meaningful
conscious activity. However, Bergson insists that
activity also depends upon real diversity. And to
prove that real diversity does take place, Bergson
points to life. As we said earlier, he associates
activity only with life and not with the material
world. If one considered only the material world,
there would be no grounds for suggesting the reality
of diversity, and idealism and mechanism would be
justified.

Later Process thought will continue to agree with
Bergson that idealism did not provide for real
diversity -- and it could not account for activity.
Of course, not all Process philosophers accepted the
idea that real activity could only be discovered in
life; or to be more specific, that real activity could
only be found in life as Bergson understood it.

A second vitalistic epistemology is that of Hans
Driesch. Of Driesch's epistemology C.D. Broad says,

> If the hypothesis of an entelechy is
> to explain anything, we must suppose

> that an entelechy is a very superior
> mind or the very superior part
> of the mind which animates the
> organism. The theory insinuates
> itself into our confidence by
> pretending that the entelechy is
> so lowly a mind as scarcely to
> deserve the name; but it can
> explain the facts only if it
> supposes the entelechy to be so
> exalted a mind as to deserve the
> name of a 'god'.5

It is too soon to comment generally on Broad's
observations. However, we can say at this point that
Driesch sees entelechy, i.e., the activity of life, as
functioning within certain limits. This is especially
true of conscious activity. To what degree this
limiting aspect of activity functions as an all
controlling god can best be discovered by looking at
what Driesch calls 'three windows into the absolute.'
The three windows are observations about reality,
which to Driesch demonstrate that some principle of
limitation is necessary, in order to account for the
fact that organisms act independently only within
certain bounds. Driesch suggests that what we call
morality cannot have developed among organisms by
sheer chance. Some principle must limit the activity
of independent organisms toward a moral order. As a
biologist Driesch cannot observe any such principle.
He sees that in all history there is the dilemma that
one should be able to show the single moral principle
behind evolution, and yet such a principle does
not show itself.7

Driesch describes his second window into the
absolute.

> The second 'window into the absolute'
> is constituted by the fact, already
> mentioned on a former occasion, that
> there is such a thing as unity of
> subjective experience in general and

106

of memory in particular; in other
words, the fact that not only
memory endures, but also something
is presented to consciousness. This
tends to prove the absolute existence of an unconscious or super-
conscious ego.8

In agreement with idealism, Driesch seems to say
that 'categories', in the Kantian sense, are necessary
in order to allow consciousness to make order out of
chaos. "Categories," says Driesch, "are brought to
consciousness by only a limited amount of acquaintance
with Givenness, but, as soon as they are brought to
consciousness, they direct consciousness in all future
experiences of Givenness; the systematization of
nature by means of categories thus becomes a
'problem'."9

Driesch does not deny that a particular stimulus
may be necessary in order to excite recognition.
However, the recognition excited appears to be out of
proportion to the stimulus. Thus there must be ideas
that are unconscious or super-conscious.

The second window suggests that there are mental
categories, and the third window suggests that there
are universals or forms.10 Together the three windows
suggest that the conscious activity of organisms is
limited by a moral principle, categories, and forms.
Yet biological evidence suggests that evolution of
organisms occurred by chance. Clearly the biological
materialism, suggested my certain interpretations of
evolution, does not explain the activity of consciousness. Broad believes that Driesch feels that the need
to explain conscious activity is more important than
accepting a materialistic interpretation of evolution.
Entelechy is precisely an illustration of the rejection
of materialistic evolutionism.

Both Bergson and Driesch agree that conscious
activity requires a principle of limitation. Driesch's
three windows into the absolute are very helpful in

explaining why this is true. However, in terms of meeting the demand for such a principle, and at the same time accounting for the diversity which neo-vitalism accepts as essential to activity, Bergson alone arrives at a well developed formulation. He concludes that duration can serve as a principle of limitation, and still participate in the universal process of events.

Bergson's use of the concept of limitation does not suggest an abstract physical principle nor a given whose content is all of reality. His use of the term duration gives it both an abstract and a concrete aspect. The fact that the unity of the past moves into the present is an abstraction. On the other hand, the past itself is a concrete unity.

Duration is for Bergson the epistemological principle of limitation for conscious activity. The perceptions or conscious activity of any mind is limited by its durational past -- often in the form of memory. This past participates in the present without preventing the present from having new relationships. Duration, of course, only applies to conscious activity. This is a further example of the dualism that is always in the background of his work.

Driesch, like Bergson, saw the need for a principle of limitation for conscious activity. That is why he said that the activity of life and mind suggests windows into the absolute. However, he was unable to develop a satisfactory formulation of that principle. Moreover, the principle for Driesch would also seem to apply only to the conscious activity of living organisms.

Both in its metaphysics and its epistemology Vitalism presented Process with a dualism. Metaphysical dualism was that of mind and matter. Epistemological dualism was between durational order of consciousness, and the probable chaos of matter.

Because conscious activity must have some principle of limitation, and because for vitalists this principle of limitation cannot be the material laws, vitalism introduced the search for a new principle of limitation for conscious activity. This principle had to allow for unity of consciousness, as well as for individual consciousnesses. However, if consciousness has a different principle of limitation than matter, we are not at a complete Process view. Nevertheless, the search for the principle of organization in conscious activity led to the development of new insights for Process.

1 Bergson. CREATIVE EVOLUTION. pp. 23-24.
2 Bergson. TIME AND FREE WILL. p. 31.
3 Bergson. CREATIVE EVOLUTION. p. 28.
4 ibid. p. 220.
5 Broad, C.D. THE MIND AND ITS PLACE IN NATURE.
    (London: Kegan, Paul, Trench, Trubner, 1923).
    p. 86.
6 Driesch. PHILOSOPHY OF ORGANISM. Vol. II, p. 361.
7 ibid. Vol. I, p. 293.   8 ibid. Vol. II, p. 362.
9 p. 307   10 p. 363.

CHAPTER XIII

SPIRITUAL EVOLUTIONISM'S
EPISTEMOLOGY

Ward and Hocking agree with Bergson that the principle of limitation must participate in the process of events, but they give a somewhat different account of this participation. Bradley, as we recall, said that we have no idea as to the outcome of the process by which the absolute whole is enriched by a plurality of conscious presentations; although he assured us that the variety of human experience must have some meaning. Bosanquet makes it clear that the significance of diversity is an important issue for all Critical Idealism, including that of Bradley's. He says, "The general formula of the Absolute, I repeat, the transmutation and rearrangement of particular experiences, and also of the contents of particular finite minds, by inclusion in a complete whole of experience, is a matter of everyday verification."[1]

Ward and Hocking, in keeping with the position of critical idealism, introduce the concept of 'individualization' in order to give meaning to finite activity and thereby try to establish diversity. Driesch, as we saw in our last Chapter, accepted the necessity of diversity, but believed that conscious activity -- entelechy -- required a principle of limitation. His attempts to explain this principle were always inconsistent with participation in free events. Ward suggests that this problem does not arise if universal conscious activity is understood to be the activity of a single conscious organism. Driesch, of course, thought of universal activity as a mere force.

The activity of any organism, as vitalism demonstrated, depends in part upon diversity. If universal conscious activity is the activity of a single organism a diversity within that organism would be required for its activity. Furthermore, if the universe is a single organism, whose activity is what we call consciousness, matter is not excluded from consciousness.

Ward, whose work we will consider first, was greatly influenced by Bradley and the Hegelian tradition. He stood with them as a general critic of materialism. His particular objection to materialism was the fact that it allowed no place for the meaningfulness of finite conscious activity. "A science," he says, "that can only offer us as its ultimate scheme of the universe the inconceivable ideal of continuous motion in an unvarying plenum, is surely as incompetent as arithmetic or geometry to furnish a concrete present-ment of a real and living world."2

Ward's anti-materialism does not mean a total rejection of all mechanistic insights about activity. He merely argues that material laws are not the source of conscious activity. Bosanquet expresses what Ward would agree are the valid insights from mechanism:

> With the externality of nature is
> bound up the conception of Mechanism.
> The essence of it is that the world
> consists of elements, complete in
> themselves, and yet determined in
> relation to elements beyond them. If
> not complete in themselves, the
> elements would be at the mercy of
> the whole, and their claims to be
> self-sufficient components would be
> gone. If not determined by others,
> the elements would not manifest even
> the appearance of entering into and
> constituting an orderly world.3

With this suggestion in mind we may look at Ward's epistemology. The chief point in his episte-mology is that finite conscious activity is meaningful because the universal consciousness is organic.4 On the highest level this implies an organic relation between God and the world, spirit and matter.

The basis of Ward's argument for the organic nature of universal consciousness is his anaylsis of human experience. Ward says,

112

We cannot, of course, recall the
beginning of our own experience,
nor can we, either by observation
or influence, attain to any conception of an experience which
would be the simplest possible.
But all that we know, directly or
indirectly, warrents the statement
that all experience is process;
not merely 'felt change', but felt
interchange. Broadly speaking
every objective change, every change
of perception, entails a subjective
change; and every subjective change,
an objective change.5

Ward is speaking of the knowing experience as an
organic unity. That is, the subject and object form
a unity in which diversity has a meaning. The new
relationship between subject and object is a new
knowing experience. Thus by calling the universal
consciousness organic, Ward is suggesting that it
provides a unity in which individual finite consciousnesses have significance. Not only does an ultimate
organic unity allow meaningful diversity, but it
actually is supposed to promote it. Self-conscious
individuality begins by the finite organism establishing itself as independent, within the unity of the
environment. For example, history, says Ward, is made
up of the unique acts and deeds of individual centers
of experience. "Further, it is not the intrinsic
nature of objects but their value for the particular
individual that immediately determines each one's
attitude towards them; and as the individuals vary, so
do their interests and pursuits.'6 However, the conscious individuality of the entity (recalling our
analysis of consciousness) is in fact the unity of the
subject and the object. With the greater degree of
individuality, there is a corresponding increase in
unity. Individuality is an increase in relations.

The movement towards unity through individualization is the limitation which organizes finite conscious

activity as a whole, and allows its contribution to the universe. But the particular unity of a given self-conscious entity is indeed something new. On one side this agrees with idealism, because the formation of unity is impossible without an absolute principle of unity.7

On the other side, this view is intended to satisfy pluralism. Ward says,

> The standpoint of pluralism in our
> day is, as we have seen, fundament-
> ally historical. It is a philosophy
> of becoming rather than being. It
> holds -- as has been said of the
> philosophy of Aristotle -- that 'the
> ultimate metaphysical explanation of
> existence must be sought not so
> much is a prius out of which things
> emerge as in the goal towards which
> they move.'8

The goal of Ward's process is an ultimate organic unity of meaningful individuals, within the single universal organism. This formulation goes ahead to speak of the development of organic unity as spiritual. An entity which reaches a high level of individual-ization may realize that relations are, in fact, internal to the cosmic organism. Such an entity would no longer need to depend on establishing its individ-uality through the setting up of independent purposes and goals, directed outside of that organism.

It is the felt interchange between subject and object that makes conscious activity possible. The individual subjects are the real diversity, proven by the fact that in consciousness they are able to est-ablish new relations. However, the object of these relations always enters into the unity, and is not known outside of a unity. The unity between subject and object is in fact the unity of the absolute consciousness itself. In all conscious experience, one experiences the Absolute.

114

According to Ward the term absolute refers to an organic unity and not to a simple unity. Finite conscious activity, made up of unity and diversity, reflects the inner nature of the absolute consciousness. Certainly this formulation provides a principle of limitation, but it is not clear that the principle of limitation remains consistent with true diversity, by participating in the process of events.

It is true that if one considers the evolution of organisms, the more complex an organism becomes the more specialized (individualized) become its parts. A highly complex organism with many very specialized parts is more unified, in that the existence of the whole organism depends upon the proper functioning of each of its parts.

In these two respects there does appear to be some analogy between the activity of a single universal organism and finite conscious activity. Up to a point the number of elements making up the consciousness of an individual entity increase that entity's awareness of itself as an individual. On the other hand, in the process of becoming an individual, an entity must become increasingly aware of its relatedness to other elements in its environment.

Ward argues that at some point the finite entity becomes aware that its individuality is merely an aspect of a single universal consciousness. With this awareness the entity no longer has need of separate individuality, but it discovers its true identity in union with the absolute whole. This outcome is completely determined, and Ward merely says that the stages in its realization are not determined.

The above must lead us to conclude that finite conscious activity is merely a temporary state in the universe. If finite conscious activity is a temporary state, it is difficult to understand how it can be considered a model for absolute consciousness. Indeed, in Ward's formulation the Absolute or principle of limitation does not seem to participate in finite

conscious activity at all, because ultimately it is not
changed by finite consciousness. The ultimate unity
will be achieved quite apart from the activity of any
particular diversity. Hocking, to whom we turn next,
speaks to this problem.

The first factor to be considered in Hocking's
position is that the absolute unity, of which Ward
spoke, is not merely a future state. Thus far we have
discussed the spiritual development as a process
toward wholeness. However, wholeness, according to
Hocking, cannot be understood as a process. What is
demanded in wholeness is something present in the now.
More specifically, the concept and meaning of wholeness is within consciousness. It is a logical
consequence of all experience. In particular terms
Hocking describes how this experience of wholeness
must be treated:

> All good things do doubtless belong
> together; but each good thing, we
> recognize, is to be pursued separately.
> The difficulty lies in inferring from
> the parts to the whole: that is to say,
> in seeing that the alternation which
> is obviously necessary as between one
> particular object and another is also
> necessary as between all particular
> objects and the whole. But just this,
> I think, is what worship means: that
> the whole must become a separate object
> of pursuit, taking its turn as if it
> also were a part, as if it were
> another among the many goods of
> practical occupation.9

Within Hocking's system, the object, which is
first established as separate from the subject, in the
act of experience, unites with the subject. Just such
a unification with the whole is the essence, according
to Hocking, of the mystical experience. The contemplation of the whole also takes place within consciousness. The absolute whole becomes our immediate object

116

of experience, and thus participates in finite consciousness.

As we said at the conclusion of our discussion on Ward, according to his formulation, the achievement of final unity through the process must represent change within the absolute consciousness, if it participates in that process. However, Ward, having rejected the idea of the absolute consciousness changing, did not clearly establish how it could participate in events. Hocking argues that for human consciousness the whole already exists as a possible object of contemplation at each instant. Therefore, the absolute whole, as object, does participate in finite consciousness, without itself changing.

We can best summarize our discussion of Ward and Hocking by drawing some connections between their positions and Bergson's position. Bergson argued that the principle of limitation participated in the temporal series of events. Its concrete content was different from instant to instant.

Ward and Hocking cannot accept Bergson's point. For them time does not change the absolute consciousness. Its concrete content always remains a unity of all reality. Their positions, taken together, suggest that the Absolute participates only spatially in events, as new organizations of its contents occur. Of course, adopting their understanding of spirit or consciousness, as ultimate reality, puts one in the rather unusual position of thinking of space being filled with 'bits of consciousness'. Yet, unlike Bergson, they do not deny absolute extension; therefore we have no alternative but to think of them as speaking of changing arrangements of consciousness in space. And clearly it could only be in such changing arrangements that the absolute consciousness participates.

So long as one is willing to accept the meaning of participation as limited to either temporal or spatial participation, both Bergson, and Ward and

Hocking, taken together, give a satisfactory explanation of how the diversity necessary for conscious activity, and the equally necessary principle of limitation, can be explained. Later we will encounter thinkers who will accept neither of the above qualifications on participation. At the moment we merely want to reaffirm the insight that conscious activity depends upon the participation of the principle of limitation in the process of events.

1 Bosanquet, B. THE PRINCIPLE OF INDIVIDUALITY AND
      VALUE. (London: Macmillan, 1912). p. 373.
2 Ward, James. NATURALISM AND AGNOSTICISM. (London:
      Adam and Charles Black, 1906). Vol. I, p.151.
3 Bosanquet. INDIVIDUALITY AND VALUE. p. 73.
4 Ward. NATURALISM AND AGNOSTICISM. Vol. II, pp.111-112
5 ibid. p. 130.
6 Ward. THE REALM OF ENDS. p. 18.
7 ibid. p. 73.   8 ibid. p. 138.
9 Hocking, William Ernest. THE MEANING OF GOD IN
      HUMAN EXPERIENCE. p. 405.

CHAPTER XIV

BERNARDINO VARISCO'S
NEO-MECHANISTIC EPISTEMOLOGY

As we have just noted, the diversity necessary
for conscious activity depends upon the principle of
limitation participating in the process of events.
Thus far, attempts to arrive at a formulation of
consciousness, which allows for the above concept,
have not been completely successful. With the exception of Bergson's, the epistemologies have suggested
that the activities of individual minds are limited by
their being understood as aspects of a single consciousness. Thus it would be more accurate to say that
individual consciousnesses participate in the principle
of limitation, rather than that the principle of limitation participates in the process of events. Such an
understanding, Broad points out, hardly agrees with the
real demand for diversity.

> The essential point is that relations
> within a mind and between its states
> seem to be different in kind from
> the relations between several minds
> and within a society, and that no
> society is at once all-inclusive and
> very highly unified. I therefore can
> see no good ground for believing in
> a single mental substance of which all
> finite minds could be regarded as
> states or modifications.1

Furthermore these essentially idealistic formulations reinforce the concept that diversity is not
ultimately real, by suggesting that a 'final' unity
within the single mental substance will be achieved.
The principle of limitation is seen as ultimately
determining activity. However, as we have explained,
there is no way to account for activity in a deterministic system. Varisco will address this point. In
his epistemology he will argue that a single consciousness may not be the principle of limitation, and that

limitation does not lead to determinism. That is, it
does not eliminate the ultimate spontaneity of individual consciousnesses. Thus activity can be
established as real, because it is consistent with the
nature of the principle of limitation.

Up to this point it has been necessary to maintain a distinction between the principle of limitation
and the concept absolute. The principle of limitation
organizes the present activity of consciousness, which
reaches an absolutely determined organization at some
future instant. In theory the principle of limitation
and the ultimate unity are the same. However, if the
nature of the former allows for activity, while the
nature of the latter represents the already determined
end of activity, the two concepts appear contradictory.
Varisco, as we will see, attempts to overcome this
problem.

He begins by establishing his firm belief that
the activity of consciousness depends upon a real
diversity. He says, "Be it observed that I do not say,
a body is a phenomenon of myself in so far as I feel
it, and therefore is nothing but a phenomenon of myself; I say, my assertion that a body is more than a
phenomenon of myself, is an assertion that extended
experience, my own and that of others, is ordered in a
certain way."2

According to Varisco reality is composed of many
centers of relatedness, called by him centers of spontaneity. They are united because they all share the
common factor of Being.3 A center of spontaneity,
which has reached the level of consciousness, is aware
of these two factors, because these factors are
inherent to it. Varisco's chief conclusion from this
analysis of consciousness is that consciousness is a
relational process of organization.4 He feels that
consciousness demands relations. An entity becomes
conscious only in relation to other centers of spon-
taneity.5

Assuming that we begin with various centers,

containing within themselves an aspect of unity, the relation of one center to another can account for the unity and diversity of conscious activity. Absolute 'ideals' used to account for unity by idealisms are unnecessary. Of course, some wider principle of unity must connect these centers, and this unity is provided by the fact that each center is capable of recognizing Being; because each center itself has Being.6

Again this argument is consistent with the requirements for conscious activity. Activity depends upon unity and diversity. Relations between centers also depend upon unity and diversity. "It is now clear," says Varisco, "that the necessity of relations completely solves the problem of reconciling unity and diversity -- of making us understand how unity and multiplicity imply each other, so that the one is impossible without the other, exists only in the other."7 Finally, relations are the constituents of knowledge, quite apart from ideals.

Being serves as a principle of limitation for consciousness, as consciousness is able to distinguish objects which contain Being from conceivable objects that do not. However, Being does not stand outside of conscious activity, but it enters into the relations between conscious centers. That is, it cannot exist apart from its recognition by minds -- it depends upon relations.8

Being is a principle of limitation required for conscious activity, but it is not free from relatedness as the term absolute applied to it might suggest. A particular finite subject, therefore, need only experience certain relations of Being in order to have consciousness. The degree of unity necessary for finite consciousness is the recognition of Being in all of those centers of spontaneity with which the particular subject interferes. Certainly, there are many centers of spontaneity with which a given subject does not interfere -- though should interference take place, Being would be recognized immediately.

121

As interference produces consciousness, we may state the above by saying that the unity needed for consciousness remains available, even if some phenomena are inside and some outside of what we know as human consciousness. Idealism, on the other hand, would insist that while something may exist outside of a particular consciousness, it has no existence outside of consciousness in general. To be outside of consciousness in general would, according to idealism, destroy unity. Idealism would argue that in Varisco's system Being as a whole must be recognized by a single consciousness, if it is to exist.

To help clarify these last two statements: Idealism, while it would admit that not everything is known by a given consciousness, would argue that the individuality of an object depends upon its being known by some consciousness. In other words ideas alone allow us to isolate an object -- to individualize it from out of the chaos of sensual impressions.

Varisco's formulation questions the possibility of a knowing subject whose concrete knowledge is all present instants of being:

> No phenomenon is possible outside
> the universal unity; if we admit
> that the universal unity is the
> consciousness of the universal
> Subject, no phenomenon is possible
> outside of the consciousness of the
> universal Subject. Just for this
> reason it must be concluded that a
> phenomenon of mine is the same, both
> as my phenomenon, and as a phenomenon
> of the universal Subject... Since a
> consciousness which is only theore-
> tical, is nothing but an abstraction,
> it is clear that if the universal
> consciousness were the unity of the
> phenomenal universe, it would not only
> be cognitive, but at the same time
> creative too. 9

He goes on to say, "The difference between a particular subject and the Universal Subject can be reduced, with reference to our present problem, to this that the first is clearly conscious of some phenomena, and the second is clearly conscious of all."10

In other words, he maintains that a universal consciousness would be the determinate cause of all finite conscious activity. However, if finite conscious activity is understood as determined, its existence cannot be explained, because it depends upon the activity of individual centers of spontaneity.

Varisco concludes that the concept of a total concrete unity of consciousness is the result of mere logical abstraction, and not of the real concrete unity of idealism's Supreme Subject. In particular, the concept of ultimate concrete unity is a logical consequence of the concept of a universe.11

His explanation for this abstraction is that its establishment is the result of a logical process innate to Being. Logically the fact that we are conscious of the establishment of finite unities, leads us to the possibility of an infinite unity. Moreover, the fact that Being itself is a constant supports the truth of this logical conclusion.12

Being, while constant, enters into the process of events because of its nature -- it relates.

> We shall never arrive, we do not say
> at the cessation of happening, but not
> even at a condition of equilibrium in
> motion, which we might compare with
> that at which our solar system,
> approximately, and not for ever, has
> arrived.
>   In fact a variation which lasts
> for ever cannot tend towards a definite
> goal, be it rest or equilibrium in
> motion. It cannot be tending toward
> it, because, if the goal were realizable

123

> it would have been realized years
> ago... That same necessity which
> makes the universe be, excludes
> the possibility of the universe,
> as wholly one, tending towards
> an end.13

In idealism the term absolute, referring to a concrete unity, implied a goal -- an end. This raises the question of whether conscious activity could be ultimately consistent with idealism's Absolute, as conscious activity requires true diversity. If activity is not consistent with the nature of the cosmos, Varisco does not see how activity can be explained. Thus the ultimate concrete unity must be a mere abstraction.

Varisco is not a teologian. However, he does present what he considers an important theological problem developing out of his work. The problem is whether the metaphysical aspect of his work should be understood as 'theistic' or 'pantheistic'. Theists, according to Varisco, are those who feel that no reason for the existence of God is necessary, and the pantheists are those who find that they must have a reason in order to allow God's existence.14

He also wonders whether there is any meaning in talking about God, if, as some pantheists suggest, the word refers to nothing more than an immanent principle. Hocking's work is some answer to Varisco's question. As we may recall, Hocking said that the 'immanent principle' is objectified for worship. God is the title given to the object of worship. Furthermore, Hocking said that worship is valuable because it produces higher morality and art. Later Chapters will also address this theological (metaphysical) problem.

In Varisco's epistemology the ultimate unity of the consciousness of the whole of Being is a logical abstraction. Nevertheless, this abstraction is grounded in the concrete reality that the Being of the universe is a constant. We are able to formulate this abstraction because of our awareness that all objects have Being. The abstraction is arrived at through the encounter with a multiplicity of objects. Unity need not be imposed upon multiplicity, but it is recognized within it. If unity is present both in individual conscious events, and also in the universe as a whole, then the whole must participate in the process of events. Furthermore, as concrete unity is reached through multiplicity, both unity and multiplicity must be factors of Being.

According to Varisco, when one speaks of 'unity' the term has a concrete and an abstract reference. For consciousness concrete unity means the unity of particular realized relations of being, and the abstract unity is the possibility of All relations of Being included in a single consciousness.

Varisco's epistemology, as summarized above, is quite different than idealism. To begin with idealism would not say that ultimate unity is an abstraction. Indeed, for idealism ultimate unity is the concrete unity of all reality. Through the activity of the individual conscious mind the concept of ideal or abstract can be formulated, but the activity involved in making this formulation is not the same as the object of that formulation. The abstract unity arrived at by conscious activity, and the ultimate concrete unity of consciousness are not the same. The former is the principle of limitation used in episte-mology to account for the unity of finite conscious-ness; the latter is the Absolute used in idealism to account for ultimate unity.

His point is that to suggest that there is any ultimate concrete unity -- an Absolute -- is to deny the very possibility of finite conscious activity. Instead, one must say that the activity of conscious-ness suggests that activity is characteristic of the universe as a whole. One may apply the term absolute to the universal activity in the sense that universal activity is part of all reality. However, in this case the term absolute would have an abstract meaning

125

as well as a concrete meaning. Abstractly the term absolute would refer to the fact that Being, while dynamic, remains a constant. The concrete reference for the term absolute could only be the particular configurations of the whole of Being at any given instant.

Such a formulation could never use the term absolute to refer to only a concrete unity. Just as the concept of principle of limitation in epistemology must allow for an abstract ideal of unity, so the use of the term absolute in metaphysics must have an abstract reference -- and not only a concrete reference as idealism would suggest. On the other hand, Varisco does not deny that the unity of consciousness has a concrete aspect, nor does he deny a concrete reference for the term absolute. His absolute is not contradictory in a system that calls for true diversity.

Varisco's position also eliminates the need for a distinction between the concepts of absolute and principle of limitation. Activity is characteristic both of individual consciousnesses and also of the universe as a whole. Universal activity may be called 'absolute' as it is a constant which includes all reality. However, one could just as well speak of concrete absoluteness as the 'principle of limitation.' Meaning, that the universal fact of Being, which permits the organization or unity of consciousness, is itself dynamic. Bergson's epistemology, we may recall, adopted just such an understanding of the concept of limitation. Varisco, unlike Bergson, finds no reason to couple epistemology with a metaphysical dualism.

1 Broad. THE MIND AND ITS PLACE IN NATURE. p. 33.
2. Varisco, Bernardino. KNOW THYSELF. trans.,
        Guglielmo Salvadori. (London: George Allen & Unwin, 1915). p. xi.

3 ibid. pp. xviii-xix. 4 p. 41. 5 p. 82.
6 p. 120. 7 p. 154. 8 p. 209.
9 pp. 227-229. 10 p. 232. 11 p. 241.
12 p. 248
13 Varisco. THE GREAT PROBLEMS. p. 245.
14 ibid. p. 357.

CHAPTER XV

EMERGENT EVOLUTIONISM'S
EPISTEMOLOGY

Varisco's explanation of how the principle of
limitation participates in the process of events
eliminated the need for making a distinction between
the activity of individual consciousnesses, and the
activity of the universe as a whole. Knowing -- one
of the activities of consciousness --, he said, was
composed of relations of interference between unified
centers of spontaneity; implying that knowledge does
not depend upon changeless ideas or forms. Likewise,
the activity of the universe as a whole is composed of
relations between Being as a constant, and the changing distributions of Being within the centers. In
other words, individual conscious activity is not
activity within the universal consciousness, but rather
it is the activity of the universe.

When Varisco discusses the activity of consciousness in his epistemology, he is also referring to his
conception of universal activity. What this formulation accomplishes is the fulfilling of both requirements for a Process epistemology. First, Being serves
as a principle of limitation for the evaluation of
mental data by allowing a mind to recognize objects
that have Being. Second, Being provides unity by its
presence in all relationships, and diversity by itself
participating in those relations.

Alexander and Morgan, as we will see, agree with
much that Varisco attempts in his formulations. That
is, they also see no reason for making a distinction
between the activity of consciousness and the organization of the universe as a whole. Nevertheless,
Varisco's suggestion that knowing means relations of
interference within Being and between centers of Being
is not the only possible way to analyze conscious
activity. What Varisco meant by the term Being, for
example, was not completely clear. Alexander with
equal success argued that consciousness can be

understood as relations of and within Space-Time. And
Morgan will offer still another alternative.

Alexander from the beginning makes it clear that
epistemology and metaphysics are not to be separated.1
As we saw in Chapter VII, Alexander selected Space-
Time, which divides itself into point-instants of space-
times, as the common stuff of reality. According to
his position, what in epistemology might be called
categories or ideals are not applicable to Space-Time,
but develop out of it.2

In other words, the categories used by the mind as
a principle of limitation for the organization of
conscious activity do not exist outside of that activity, but arise from within the activity itself.
Another way of stating this is to say that the principle of limitation participates in the process of
events. Conscious mental activity is an aspect of
some universal activity, the organization of which is
the principle of limitation. Alexander says, "Our
hypothesis is merely that alike in the matrix of finite
things and in all finite things there is something of
which, on the highest level we know of finite exis-
tents, mind is the counterpart or correspondent."3

Furthermore, Alexander understands that the
participation of the principle of limitation in the
process of events accounts for both unity and
diversity.4 The factor which unifies all entities,
according to Alexander, is that they are all spatiotemporal configurations of Space-Time. Yet as Space-
Time is itself divided into space-times, each entity
has its own esse. In other words, diversity is characteristic of the principle of limitation itself, i.e.,
the universal organization of the activity of Space-
Time. The activity of consciousness, which requires
both unity and diversity, is the same as the nature of
the universe as a whole.

Having established that Alexander understands that
the requirements for conscious activity are a principle
of limitation, and that principle's participation in

the process of events, which allows for unity and for diversity, we must next look at how he understands knowing. For Varisco, we may recall, knowing was the recognition of Being through the interferences between spontaneous centers. Alexander will argue that knowledge results from what he calls a 'selection' of objects by a mind. Values are the basis for this so called selection.

A mind for Alexander is an extremely complex organization of Space-Time having the quality of consciousness. A living cell or an atom would be illustrations for less complex configurations. Alexander is suggesting that the process of knowing requires that the subject be a mind. He would not, for example, say that one atom 'knows' another atom. The activity to which we give the name consciousness does not occur until a certain level of complexity has emerged within the universal process.5

Qualities such as truth, goodness and beauty can be experienced only in the cognitive act of unity between a conscious subject and its object. These qualities Alexander also calls values, and they are mental.

> But their dependence on mind does not
> deprive them of reality. On the con-
> trary, they are a new character of
> reality, not in the proper sense
> qualities at all, but values, which
> arise through the combination of mind
> with its object. What experience of
> every kind is thought to be, namely,
> something in which the mind and its
> objects can be distinguised but can-
> not be separated, so that there can
> be no space nor color without an
> experiencing mind, is true of values
> but nowhere before.6

Because of the very nature of reality, the complexity of relations in Space-Time, on the level of human consciousness, have the special significance of creating values through the combination of mind with its objects. Furthermore, the development of values is a social action of the unity among knowing subjects.7

Morality is produced by the interaction between man as a society and his environment. "Accordingly it is indifferent to say that morality is the adaptation of human action to the environment under social conditions, or that it is the system of actions approved by man under the conditions set by his own envirnoment."8 Either way it is the very nature of reality to form a complex unity that leads to morality.

Morality is for Alexander a third kind of quality. He first admitted the existence of primary and secondary qualities. The secondary qualities are the ways in which a conscious mind perceives space-times. The primary qualities are common to both subject and object. However, these two kinds of qualities must be seen along with values. Values are a complex-unity. They exist only because of a unity, but their independence is real along with that unity. This is a level of perception limited to self-conscious minds. It is a product of the complexity of space-times which are the mental configurations.9 All three kinds of qualities serve as principles of limitation.

For Alexander, the unique aspect of self-conscious life, -- the assignment of values -- has both an external as well as an internal aspect. Values are both public and private. They are private in that they depend upon individual conscious minds. They are also public in that morality is value in a social setting. We must remember that while the recognition of values requires a conscious mind (and morality requires a society of conscious minds) values are recognized -- just as Varisco's Being is recognized -- and not 'created' by the mind.10

Here, as in Varisco, the unity of the knowing process is understood as having an abstract as well as a concrete content. The concrete aspect is the particular value selected by individual minds. On the other hand, the abstract aspect is a logical concept of returning to unity, which Alexander has just called 'adaptation'. The point of adaptation is that as knowledge of certain concrete values is possible for finite minds, and as the social unity of values leads to a moral society, then it is abstractly possible to conceive a single mind that knows all values and is moral to the highest possible degree.

God is the entity whose perspective includes knowledge of all finite values, and who is moral to the highest possible degree. This abstract concept of God is a way of describing the principle of limitation necessary for the whole of consciousness, because it suggests the ultimate organization of values. However, as the principle of limitation participates in the process of events, God is affected by finite values.11 God always participates in values, and always represents the best possible morality. No possibility exists which is better than the possibility offered by Deity.

We have now presented two systems in terms of the way in which they contribute to the requirements of a Process epistemology. For our purposes, one great difficulty in clarifying these systems has been the establishment of the precise connection between metaphysical and epistemological formulations. Of course, the connection between reality and knowing is always a mixture of metaphysical and epistemological questions. The attempt to mark a rigid division between the two is never satisfactory. For Process, one consideration remains paramount. There must be no point in the metaphysical-epistemological system at which true unity or true diversity is denied; or where the one or the other becomes unnecessary or inconsistent.

The idealisms discussed in earlier Chapters were inconsistent with Process because their Absolute had different meanings in reference to metaphysics and epistemology. In metaphysics the term absolute

referred to the ultimate concrete unity of all reality.
In epistemology, on the other hand, the term absolute
referred to the principle of limitation which provided
organization for conscious activity. In the former
absoluteness precluded true diversity, while in the
latter absoluteness assumed diversity.

In Varisco's and Alexander's systems the above
distinction is not followed. They both assume that
absolute has only a single reference for both metaphysics and epistemology. The term absolute refers to
an ultimate principle having two aspects. The first
aspect is a logically abstract aspect of total unity.
This aspect is abstract in the sense that a final unity
which precludes diversity is not realized. However,
the fact that ultimate concrete unity is an abstraction
does not make it meaningless. In spite of its abstract
nature absolute unity serves both metaphysics and
epistemology as a principle of limitation. Without it
activity would appear chaotic. In principle idealism's
concept of limitation is the same as the concept of an
abstract understanding of an absolute unity. However,
idealism also realized that, unless the absolute
concretely contains all reality, change in the Absolute
becomes possible, as it would be subject to participation in the process of events. This last point
proves to be true. When the total unity is abstract,
it does not preclude the concrete existence of lesser
unities.

Indeed the second aspect of the term absolute, as
it is used by Varisco and Alexander, is that it must
be understood along with a concept of its division into
concrete unities, i.e. a multiplicity of entities.
True diversity means that entities have an aspect of
unity in themselves. Otherwise, they would be determined by some absolute principle of unity. As the
unity of each entity has its source out from the
ultimate principle, one can equally well think of the
concrete aspect of unity as being the total concrete
content of all entities. As the concrete content of
entities change, the unity participates in this
conscious process.

An attempt to maintain a consistent belief in true unity and true diversity through both metaphysics and epistemology is characteristic of both Varisco's and Alexander's systems. Therefore, their formulations are of great use to the development of Process. Indeed the usefulness to Process of these formulations becomes clearer if we look at the work of C. Lloyd Morgan.

Morgan, as we saw in Chapter VII, selected Alexander as a target for attack. Both men were emergent evolutionists, and thus shared much in common. But some of Alexander's concepts seemed to Morgan to disagree with the data coming from biology. Morgan, in particular, believed that biologically understood the activity of mind must be grounded in phenomena. He says, "I seek in vain for evidence that spatio-temporal relatedness does exist apart from physical events."12

In other words, Morgan argues that all forms of knowing are states within mind's structure. "My doctrine is," he says, "that all that is minded is within us, and founded primarily on the correlated outcome of receptor-patterns; that there are physical things in their own right outside us in a non-mental world; and that the properties which render them objective in mind are projiciently referred to these things."13

Projicient reference is the special relatedness established between objects and the human subject, by way of the physical structures composing the subject. As an illustration of the necessity of the structure, many of the human mental activities depend upon the special form of the human visual development. What Morgan wants to know, for example, is how one can say that the elements of consciousness are in all reality, when consciousness, as we know it, seems intimately related to the 'chance' development of the human eye. Driesch, another biologist, we may recall, pointed out that while consciousness demanded some principle of limitation which ordered activity, organisms themselves appeared to have evolved through a

process of chance. Morgan reinforces this point by
suggesting that what we call consciousness could not
exist apart from the particular structures of
conscious organisms. Consciousness is the way certain
organisms relate to their environment. Consciousness
is in no sense a characteristic of the environment
itself apart from the structure of knowing subjects."14

Alexander, on the other hand, suggested that
consciousness was a characteristic of a particular
configuration of Space-Time. And Morgan interpreted
Alexander as suggesting that consciousness can be
understood apart from the physical structures of the
organism. This he cannot accept.

> If the idealists assert that color
> lives only at the top, in the mind,
> irrespective of physical correlates
> in the organism; or if the realist
> assert that it lives only at the
> bottom, in the thing, irrespective
> of the physical correlates
> in the organism; I respectfully
> submit that each goes beyond the
> evidence. According to the evi-
> dence (if I do not misread it) color
> lies in the whole situation; in
> other words, it has being by virtue
> of extrinsic relatedness of person
> (mind-body) and thing... And if
> either person or thing, which thus
> function as extrinsic terms, be absent
> there is no color (as Mr. Alexander
> admits there is no beauty) in being.15

On the one hand Morgan admits that conscious
activity must have some principle of organization.
On the other hand, consciousness is peculiar to the
brain's structure in the sense that vision is peculiar
to the eye. The structure of the eye allows for
vision, and the structure of the brain allows for
consciousness. Similar to Driesch, Morgan concludes
that the existence of 'values' is the one thing that

136

shows the need to posit some plan of organization for consciousness.

Since Morgan rejects Alexander's position that values are characteristic of Space-Time itself, he offers the alternative that values,-- the plan of consciousness-- are instinctive aspects of heredity.16

> Objective values, as such, may be
> regarded as the items of stuff
> which in our present context con-
> stitute a schema, or that which is
> schematized in reflective thought.
> The substantial going together in
> this distinctive manner of these
> items of value within the schema is
> that which gives it worth.17

By the term 'objective' Morgan is suggesting that values are not limited to individual minds. Values for Morgan are a special sort of relatedness possible only for minds on the level of emergence called 'reflective reference'. These values are not predetermined totally, but are conditioned by such factors as the physical and social environment, and the needs, structure and health of the body.

In Morgan's analysis, as was true in Driesch's, we appear to reach a point at which the organization of conscious activity, and the biological evidence for the chance nature of evolution are contradictory. The fact that values form an objective schema indicates that conscious activity is capable of organization. Nevertheless, evolutionary activity appears to be random in its total effects. Therefore, Morgan next gives his account for why random activity is found to be organized within certain emergent levels -- especially within the conscious level. Morgan's resolution of this dilemma stems from his introduction of a doctrine of God. According to Morgan, God cannot be proven to exist, but God's existence does create a complete system.18 Concerning belief he says,

This implies the emergence of the
religious attitude, that is, a
mental attitude, toward the acknow-
ledged reality of Divine Purpose.
It is this mental attitude that is
in some persons emergent... And in
this sense the rational order of the
cosmos, no less than Divine Purpose,
is dependent on mind. But under
acknowledgement we believe, though
we are unable to prove to the satisfaction of those who do not believe
(1) that the rational order has being
independently of the reflective mind
that is evolved within it, and (2)
that Divine Purpose has being independently of the spiritual attitude
through which it is revealed in this
or that individualized person.19

In the above quotation Morgan begins by rein-
forcing his point that no organization of activity into
what we call consciousness exists apart from the
physical structure of brains. However, he also feels
that there is sufficient evidence to support 'belief'
that rational order has at least an aspect which is
independent of the physical structure. In particular,
the fact that conscious minds share values indicates
some order beyond that of individual minds. He goes on
to say,

But possession by mind implies for
Mr. Alexander, 'combination of mind
with its object' or, in my phrase-
ology, copresence of enjoyment with
reflective reference. Enjoyment is
purely individual; and yet even this
enjoyment in presence of value is,
as Mr. Alexander insists, more than
individual, it is communal. Reference
is no less individual; it is social
and hence, as I think, so far personal.20

In order to understand the above we must look very closely at the distinction between individual and personal. Individuality is admitted to be characteristic of an entity itself. Personality is the character of an entity achieved through its relation to other entities.21 In other words, Morgan suggests that conscious entities have two aspects. On the one hand they are individual -- absolutely unique. This concept would clearly be consistent with evolution by chance events, in which the probability of even two organisms being the same is infinitely small. On the other hand, conscious entities are personal -- relative. That is, entities on any level of emergence share characteristics. The shared characteristics suggest some cosmic plan -- or, for those persons who have a religious attitude, a 'divine purpose'.

Like individual entities the cosmic plan or divine purpose also has two aspects. On the one hand, as Morgan said, the divine purpose has being independently of the spiritual attitude through which it is revealed in this or that individual person. On the other hand it is relative by being dependent on mind. It, like mind, is bi-polar. Finally like the reflective mind the cosmic plan is a rational order.

Of course, Morgan said that his conclusions in favor of a divine purpose were not subject to proof. Accepting that situation, if they are 'believed' the metaphysical implications of Morgan's system would have marked similarities with the metaphysical implications of Varisco's and Alexander's systems.

It will help our understanding if we mention some of these possible similarities. First, the absolute pole on the level of mind and on the divine level allows relatedness. And, the absolute pole does serve as a principle of limitation. On the human level it permits the establishment of values, and on the divine level universals. Values, we may recall, are the interpretation of events relative to the individuality of the conscious entity's structure or configuration. Values provide a standard by which entities can evaluate events. On the level of God, we may assume that universals are the divine evaluation of events. Morgan, like Alexander, would certainly assume that God enjoyed a wider perspective than any human consciousness.

Second, not only is the absolute pole a principle of limitation, but for Morgan it must also participate in the process of events. According to Morgan the individuality of the entity depends upon its relations with other entities. Furthermore, we are told that the divine purpose depends on finite minds. Relations on the level of minds are possible through reflective reference to universal characteristics. However, universal characteristics also depend for their emergence upon finite minds.22 From the viewpoint of metaphysics he might conclude with Alexander that individual conscious minds represent a division of a universal principle of consciousness -- but not of Space-Time. Moreover, that division is a true diversity, as the universal consciousness would participate in the process of events. Once again in Morgan's formulations we have observed the essential requirements for a Process epistemology.

His epistemology demonstrates some differences from Alexander's. The most important difference is Morgan's grounding of consciousness in physical events. This was done, as we saw, in order to incorporate data coming out of the study of evolution.

Morgan's point has been that the particular nature of consciousness could not have existed until the chance evolution of the physical structure of the conscious organism. If the human organism had not evolved, then consciousness would never have come about. Morgan believes that Alexander's thinking suggests that the nature of the universe itself predetermined the necessary development of an organism with the human mind. Of course, Alexander did not suggest that particular minds were predetermined, but it is true that he implies that something like the human mind had to evolve.

In Chapter VII we noted that Alexander said that the levels of emergence were predetermined, even though the particular entities on each level were not. Morgan rejected even the determination of the levels. From a metaphysical viewpoint, Morgan's use of biological data established the total participation of the principle of limitation in the process of events. According to Morgan, we must assume that the principle of limitation did not even exist until physical events began to occur. At the outset activity was free; it was 'pure' potential to use Bergson's term. The fact that events occurred as they did was sheer chance; but once they began to occur the principle of limitation developed.

Varisco and Alexander would agree that the principle of limitation always existed abstractly, but that its concrete content developed. Morgan, on the other hand, has suggested that the principle of limitation could not have existed before physical events. The absolute and relative poles must always be found together.

According to Morgan the biological perspective demands the conclusion that conscious activity is sheer chance. Morgan's introduction of God is used as an argument in favor of the metaphyscial view that some ultimate principle underlies the fact that the universe is active rather than entropic. He does not say that sheer chance can finally explain why there is activity rather than no activity. However, every concrete form of activity -- including conscious activity-- must be assumed to exist because of sheer chance; if one takes the biological evidence seriously. The above point may be restated by saying: 'Anything which now is, might equally well not have been.' The fact of consciousness is the result of chance evolution.

Making consciousness the result of chance means that consciousness is itself a chance event. Process will now consider whether its only means of achieving a consistent formulation of true diversity lies in the assumption that consciousness is the result of chance rather than of purpose in even the most limited sense of that term.

1 Alexander. SPACE, TIME AND DEITY. Vol. I, p. 7.
2 ibid. p. 190.   3 vol. II, p. 44.
4 pp. 94-95   5 p. 238.   6 p. 244.
7 p. 261.   8 p. 274.   9 p. 282.
10 p. 311.   11 p. 400.
12 Morgan. EMERGENT EVOLUTION. p. 23.
13 ibid. p. 50.   14 pp. 183-184. 15 p. 229.
16 Morgan, C. Lloyd. LIFE, MIND AND SPIRIT. (London:
     Williams & Norgate, 1926). p. 146.
17 ibid. p. 262. 18 p. 299.   19 pp. 303-304.
20 p. 310.   21 p. 310.
22 Morgan. EMERGENT EVOLUTION. p. 209.

CHAPTER XVI

TEILHARD DE CHARDIN'S
EPISTEMOLOGY

Grounded as he is in the sciences, Teilhard, like
Driesch and Bergson and Morgan, sees that some principle of limitation is needed in order to explain the
organization of activity. A part of this demand comes
from the fact that the process of evolution confronts
the scientist with what appear to be random events.
This dilemma applies to the activity of consciousness,
of which Teilhard says; "The consciousness of each of
us is evolution looking at itself and reflecting upon
itself."1

Teilhard observes that he accepted the random
nature of evolutionary activity for a long time, before becoming aware of any possibility of overall
organization of that activity. He tells us that his
first thought of such organization came as a revelation:

> As I listened to my friend my heart
> began to burn within me and my mind
> awoke to a new and higher vision of
> things. I began to realize vaguely
> that the multiplicity of evolutions
> into which the world-process seems
> to us to be split up is in fact
> fundamentally the working out of
> one single great mystery; and this
> first glimpse of light caused me, I
> know not why, to tremble in the
> depths of my soul.2

This insight about activity certainly applies to
conscious activity, but not only to conscious activity,
as many idealists would maintain. "A mankind which
proclaims that it is alone, or in a special position,
in the universe reminds us of the philosopher who
claims to reduce the whole of the real to his own
consciousness, so exclusively as to deny true existence

143

to other men."3

The connection between Teilhard's new insight concerning activity in general, and its application to conscious activity is suggested in the following:

> The most extraordinary thing about
> the phenomenon of knowledge is not
> that each one of us can understand
> the world. The really amazing thing
> is that the countless points of view
> represented by our individual thoughts
> should have a point of coincidence;
> that, intellectually, we should all
> appreciate one and the same pattern
> in the universe; that we should
> understand one another. The reason
> for the existence of this mutual
> understanding, of this intellectual
> concurrence in our collective
> penetration of the real, can be
> found only in the existence of a
> principle which controls and unifies
> individual perceptions.4

In other words, conscious activity reinforces the demand for some principle of organization or limitation. Up to this point in the argument Morgan and Teilhard would be in close agreement. However, Morgan seemed to suggest that the principle of limitation, i.e., the dynamic organization of the universe, had no existence prior to physical events. The problem which Morgan's concept presents is how to account for the fact that activity began at all, if activity in part depends upon a principle of limitation, and yet there may have been a time when that principle did not exist. Of course, Morgan admits that activity suggests that some principle of organization did always exist, even if that point is beyond conclusive proof.

Teilhard believes that the fact of activity itself is conclusive proof for a primordial principle of limitation. He expresses a total commitment to the idea of a necessary principle of limitation which made the beginning of organized activity possible.5 This concept leads him to the further conclusion of the necessity of having "faith in a final completion of all things." Neither Driesch nor Morgan suggest such an idea. Therefore, we would do well to investigate how it arose for Teilhard.

Teilhard believed that the biological evidence for evolution not only suggested a necessary principle of limitation, but it also demonstrated that the nature of that principle could be known. He says, "It is one in which the consistence of the elements and their stability of balance lie in the direction not of matter but of spirit; in such a universe, we must remember, that the fundamental property of the cosmic mass is to concentrate upon itself, within an ever-growing consciousness, as a result of attraction or synthesis."6

He also believed that each step in evolution, no matter how random it may appear, had a factor in common with every other step. Evolution as a whole represents a process of the concentration of activity around centers of increasing synthesis. Consciousness, for example, illustrates an extreme concentration of activity around a given point of reference. This reference is described by Teilhard as the 'morals' of a particular conscious organism. We will say more about the concept of morals in a moment.

The ultimate centralization of universal activity, according to Teilhard, occurs at point Omega. This belief in the outcome of evolution does not, he says, contradict the random nature of some evolutionary activity. "Nevertheless, for all the control exercised by the polarizing action of Omega, convergence is effected only by a means of divergencies that allow life to try everything."7

His principle of limitation appears to function at the beginning, during, and at the end of the pro-cess of events. However, the principle does not prevent diversity. The fact of diversity continues to be accepted even though Teilhard associates the principle of limitation with the concept of God.8

Up to this time men who have met the requirements of a Process epistemology have done so by suggesting that the principle of limitation can allow diversity only if it participates in the process of events. Whether or not Teilhard accepted such participation of the principle is not yet clear. We can point out a potential problem that the Teilhardian system has for the establishment of such participation by the principle.

If the goal of the process of events is determined by the principle of limitation before the process even begins, then it would seem impossible for any events to have significant meaning for the process. This, we may recall, was the gist of the problem which Bradley had with the Hegelian system. Clearly Teilhard sees the need for diversity. The problem is the establishment of the meaningfulness of that diversity.

We can begin here by looking at the nature of diversity in conscious activity. According to Teilhard, conscious minds gain their individuality from a particular kind of social relatedness. He calls this relatedness 'responsibility'.

> From this point of view, and as a rough initial description, we may say that the evolution of responsibility is simply one particular aspect of cosmogenesis. Or to put it more exactly, it is cosmogenesis itself observed and measured not (as we customarily do) by degree of organic complexity or psychic change, but by the degree of constantly increasing interinfluence within a multitude which is progressively concentrated upon itself in a convergent medium.9

In keeping with this line of thought, Teilhard says,

> In other words Evolution in
> <u>rebounding</u> reflectively upon it-
> self, acquires <u>morality</u> for the
> purpose of its further advance.
> In yet other terms, and whatever
> anyone may say, above a certain
> level, technical progress neces-
> sarily and functionally adds
> moral progress to itself.10

Once evolution has reached the reflective level,
i.e., the level of consciousness, advances cease to
be achieved by the 'degree of organic complexity of
psychic change.' In other words, individual entities
stop forming organic unities, in which the nature of
the unity is dominate over the diversity that it
includes. Instead individual conscious entities
'inter-influence' one another. That is, they relate
to one another in a bond of mutual 'responsibility'
without the loss of their individuality.

For Teilhard morality represents the unity of
conscious individuals. Like the formation of the
organic unities on the lower levels of evolution, the
moral unity comes about only by trial and error. Evils
are those unsuccessful attempts at morality. Such
attempts become 'dead-ends' in the process that is
evolution. They are unsuccessful adaptations, to put
it in Alexander's terms.11 The 'convergent medium',
of which Teilhard spoke, is also called by him the
'noosphere'.12

Until evolution reaches the level of consciousness true diversity does not become apparent. At the
outset the principle of limitation does predetermine
the stages of evolution. On the material level
activity is mechanistic. Out of this mechanistic
activity comes life, which hints at the potential for
the development of true diversity. Only on the level
of consciousness do true individuals emerge. Teilhard
uses the term 'love' to designate the final unity of

consciousness.13   God is also called Love.14

Teilhard was of the opinion that the type of unity
illustrated by the complexity of conscious individuals
in the noosphere is somehow superior to the unity of
the cosmos which existed prior to the emergence of
consciousness. Therefore, unity as a principle of
limitation does participate in the process of events
to the extent that it is 'perfected' by these events.

Granted that Teilhard's thought is difficult to
follow, the foregoing analysis does seem to show that
he tried to meet the requirements for a Process
epistemology. First, he clearly saw the need for a
principle of limitation. Second, his suggestion that
the development of conscious individuals perfected the
principle of limitation shows that he held that the
diversity could only be real if the principle of limitation participated in the process of events.

Nevertheless, Teilhard, somewhat like Hegel,
adopts two different understandings of the concept
absolute. For epistemology he speaks in terms of a
principle of limitation which he called responsibility
or morality. This principle directs consciousness
toward relationships, by serving as the basis upon
which conscious entities are united. Clearly morals
are not unlike Varisco's Being or Alexander's values
in their role as a principle of limitation.

On the metaphysical level, the principle of limitation becomes an absolute concrete unity of all
reality. This unity is clearly not the same as the
Hegelian Absolute. Hegel suggested that diversity
finally vanished into concrete unity. Teilhard said
that ultimate concrete unity remains a complexity of
individuals.

In support of Teilhard's position, it is true
that, using the model of an organism, one can speak of
complex-unity. However, these organic unities are
never ultimate, as the individual entities composing
an organism continue to produce changes in the

organism as a whole. But Teilhard does not speak of the ultimate unity as organic.

Contrarywise, he suggests that Omega -- which is called ultimate -- should not be thought of as the point at which the universe becomes a single conscious organism. Instead, taking his description of the noosphere as something like a model for Omega, we might think of Omega as a perfect society in which the individuality of each entity is determined totally by its feelings of moral responsibility for all other entities. This probable view of Omega is also supported by the fact that evils, according to Teilhard, are unsuccessful attempts at morality, and are dead-ends in evolution. If Omega is the only successful outcome of evolution, it must be free of evils, i.e., perfectly moral. Even Teilhard admits that diversity is the result of trial and error. If errors cease to be made at point Omega, it is very difficult to understand the basis for a diversity.

The point is that many of the references to Omega imply that it is the ultimate determination of reality. In which case it would be contradictory to true diversity, and its formulation would represent an understanding of absoluteness that is not acceptable to Process thought, or to organic philosophy in general.

1 Teilhard. THE PHENOMENON OF MAN. p. 244.
2 Teilhard de Chardin. HYMN OF THE UNIVERSE. (London: Collins, 1965). p.50.
3 Teilhard de Chardin. CHRISTIANITY AND EVOLUTION. (London: Collins, 1971). p. 43.
4 ibid. p. 61.
5 Teilhard. HUMAN ENERGY. p. 139.
6 Teilhard. CHRISTIANITY AND EVOLUTION. p. 87.
7 Teilhard. ACTIVATION OF ENERGY. p. 124.

8 Teilhard. HUMAN ENERGY. p. 109.
9 Teilhard. ACTIVATION OF ENERGY. p. 209.
10 Teilhard de Chardin. THE FUTURE OF MAN. trans.,
     Norman Denny. (London: Collins, 1964).
11 Teilhard. ACTIVATION OF ENERGY. p. 108.
12 ibid. p. 144.
13 Teilhard. HUMAN ENERGY. p. 83.
14 ibid. p. 68.

CHAPTER XVII

A.N. WHITEHEAD'S
EPISTEMOLOGY

A Process epistemology requires first of all a principle of limitation for consciousness. Second it requires that conscious activity -- like all other activity -- must be composed of true unity and true diversity. In the epistemologies which we have considered, the principle of limitation provides the unity or the organization necessary for conscious activity.

As we have seen time and again, the concept of unity is directly related to the concept of absoluteness. In idealistic philosophy the term Absolute generally refers to an ultimate concrete unity of all reality. Within an ultimate concrete unity activity ceases to exist because diversity is no longer possible. For the idealistic philosophers, who understand the Absolute to be an ultimate concrete unity, the abstract unity provided for conscious activity by the principle of limitation and the unity of the Absolute are different. The former allows for real diversity, but the latter does not.

Process philosophers have argued that these two understandings of unity make the concept ambiguous. If unity allows for diversity, this must be true in the cosmos as a whole and also in finite consciousnesses. Otherwise, the 'source' of conscious activity cannot be explained. Of course, if unity allows for diversity this means that its concrete content cannot be all of reality.

One of the important tasks for Process epistemologies has been an attempt to discover the nature of the principle of limitation, if one rejects the concept that it parallels an ultimate unity of all reality. The most common solution has been the suggestion that the absolute unity divides itself into a multiplicity of entities. Thus each entity is both a unity in itself, and also a participant in a common principle of unity shared by all entities. Consciousness is possible because one entity is able to recognize another entity and at the same time maintain its own individuality. Another way of making this point is to say that the absolute unity participates in the activity of consciousness.

In these epistemologies the term absolute has two references or aspects. Its abstract reference is an ideal about a single consciousness that, unlike any finite consciousness, is always aware of the totality of conscious events. Its concrete reference is a present unity composed of those conscious events which have already occurred. As conscious events continue to occur, the concrete reference of the absolute changes, while the abstract reference remains the same.

That events occur in consciousness is accepted by both idealistic and Process philosophers. The former, however, cannot account for the source of conscious activity, as the concrete content of their Absolute is a unity of all reality. Process thinkers, on the other hand, have argued that, because primordial unity has divided itself, the activity which results from the factors of unity and diversity produces concrete changes within the cosmos.

Using the model of an organism for the cosmos, it can be argued that cosmic activity is comparable to changes within a finite organism that are brought about by new relations among its parts. These new relations change the concrete nature of the organism, while abstractly that organism remains the same.

In order for consciousness to occur, by the Process model thus far presented, there must be objects for consciousness, i.e., a diversity; and consciousness must both be changed by its relations to objects and also abstractly remain the same. In other words, consciousness must be composed of events -- relations. The formulation that we have outlined continues to have a serious problem with the term absolute. If, as has been suggested, all activity occurs within an

organic unity, then there is nothing outside of that
unity. A strict analogy between the cosmic organism
and a finite organism or consciousness becomes
impossible. We know of no independent organism or
free consciousness, as understood by Process, whose
inner activity does not depend upon external objects.
Indeed for Process thought it is always directly or
indirectly in response to the external objects that
internal activity originates. If one is to maintain
the organic or consciousness model for the universe,
one must consider the issue of the cosmic organism
relating to something external from itself. Thus far
we have only spoken of the cosmic organism relating to
its own internal structure.

On the other hand, if the cosmic organism has
external objects, it could not even be considered a
unity of all reality abstractly, and diversity would
have to be something other than a division of the
absolute unity itself. What we are now discussing is
partly a metaphysical problem. As we have seen,
Process demands that true unity and diversity be
consistently maintained through metaphysics and also
epistemology. If finite conscious activity requires
external objects, the point must be considered that
this might also be true for the cosmic consciousness.

Whitehead is the most successful of all Process
thinkers in establishing a single understanding of
the universal process which applies equally well to
finite consciousnesses and to a single universal
consciousness. We begin our consideration of Whitehead
by looking at his analysis of finite consciousness.

His most concise analysis of finite consciousness
is to be found in his brief work SYMBOLISM ITS MEANING
AND EFFECT. Here he describes conscious experience as
being composed of two things symbols and meanings.

> There are no components of experience
> which are only symbols or only mean-
> ings... This statement is the foun-
> dation of a thoroughgoing realism.

153

> It does away with any mysterious
> element in our experience which is
> merely meant, and thereby behind
> the veil of direct perception. It
> proclaims the principle that
> symbolic reference holds between
> two components in a complex experi-
> ence, each intrinsically capable of
> direct recognition. Any lack of
> such conscious analytical recog-
> nition is the fault of the defect
> in mentality on the part of a
> comparatively low grade percipient.1

The above clearly demonstrates that Whitehead
holds conscious activity to be composed of unity and
diversity. Consciousness, he says, is a complex
experience -- a unity -- among components. Furthermore, he is suggesting that a principle of limitation
participates in the process of conscious events. In
particular, he says that each entity is 'intrinsically'
capable of direct 'recognition'. That is, factors in
a conscious event are both related to each other and
somehow independent. The following is a greater
clarification of the unity-diversity concept:

> Our perception is not confined to
> universal characters; we do not
> perceive disembodied color or disem-
> bodied extensiveness; we perceive the
> wall's color and extensiveness...
> This concrete relationship is a
> physical fact which may be very
> unessential to the wall and very
> essential to the percipient. The
> spatial relationship is equally
> essential both to wall and per-
> cipient; but the color side of the
> relationship is at the moment indif-
> ferent to the wall, though it is
> part of the make-up of the percipient.
> In this sense, and subject to their
> spatial relationships, contemporary

events happen independently. I
call this type of experience
'presentational immediacy'. It
expresses how contemporary events
are relevant to each other, and
yet preserve a mutual independence.2

There are several factors involved in the above
illustration: (i) The sense data involved in any
perception depend both on the percipient organism and
on its spatial relations to the perceived organism;
(ii) The contemporary world is exhibited as extended
and as a plenum of organisms; (iii) Presentational
immediacy is an important factor only in the experience
of a few high-grade organisms.3 To restate these
observations; First, the values of any specific sense-
data depend both upon the subject and the object being
unique individuals. Second, extensiveness, required
for perception, is a common factor for both the subject and the object. Third, conscious activity depends
upon there being a mind participating in the event.

Having demonstrated that Whitehead holds that
conscious activity is composed of unity and diversity,
we must next look at how the principle of limitation
functions for the conscious mind. One factor of
limitation has already been mentioned; namely, that all
entities share extensiveness. Another factor of
limitation is time. According to Whitehead, time is
bi-polar. First it is concrete succession of events
in which the later state exhibits conformity to the
antecedent state. Second, time is an abstract
succession of the whole of the past into the whole of
the present.4

In other words the consciousness of finite mind
is limited by both the extensiveness of entities and
the temporal events of the past. Time, like space,
is a unity. It is durational in the Bergsonian sense.
Unity exists within the conscious entity as well as
between entities. Whitehead's name for temporal unity
is 'causal-efficacy'. Again, like Bergson's duration,
it is limited to high-grade, i.e., self-conscious

organisms.5

It is the particular past of an organism that contributes to its unique individual perceptions. Here Whitehead would be somewhat in agreement with Morgan's epistemology. A part of the organism's temporal past is its evolutionary emergence. The physical structure of the conscious organism has a direct role in perception.6 Indeed it is the structure of the organism's own body that represents the unity between itself and the structure of its object.7

The unity between subject and object is the limitation imposed by the particular spatial relationships between the structure of the subject and its object. On the other hand, the unity within the subject and object is their particular temporal pasts. Whitehead's formulation suggests that the concept of unity has two parts; both parts allowing for diversity. The spatial unity is divided into entities, each of which have extensiveness. This suggests the spatial limitation divides itself into centers, and thus participates in spatial events. On the other hand, there is temporal unity which appears to be somehow different for each conscious entity. It is a unity if the entity through its past, and serves consciousness as a principle of limitation.

It would be quite easy to jump to the conclusion that for Whitehead, as for Alexander, the term absolute or concept of principle of limitation refers to Space-Time. However, there has been no clear suggestion that either space or time is absolute. Each conscious entity has its own space and its own time. While both space and time appear to serve as principles of limitation for conscious activity, it is not yet sure how overall unity is achieved in the universe. The temporal unity of the individual consciousnesses, which certainly suggests that the principle of limitation participates in events, does not explain the nature of the unity between consciousnesses. Unless this latter sort of unity is explained, the principle of limitation has not been described.

We must see how Whitehead's epistemology ties
into his metaphysics. Whitehead says, "It is the
task of philosophic speculation to conceive the happen-
ings of the universe so as to render understandable
the outlook of physical science and to combine this
outlook with the direct persuasions representing the
basic facts upon which epistemology must build."8 A
significant portion of Whitehead's writings are
devoted to demonstrating why his analysis of conscious
activity does in fact agree with his metaphysical
system; which metaphysic is built up not only from
the data of the field of epistemology, but also from
data coming out of the special sciences, e.g., biology,
physics. In the Introduction to PROCESS AND REALITY
Whitehead says, "Indeed, if this cosmology be deemed
successful, it becomes natural at this point to ask
whether the type of thought involved be not a trans-
formation of some main doctrines of Absolute Idealism
onto a realistic basis."9 This quotation helps to
show how very central epistemology is for Whiteheadian
thought. Clearly, it is appropriate to look at his
work in terms of other epistemologies of his day.

    The first Whiteheadian suggestion for us to
consider is that all reality must be understood as a
single process. Whitehead argues that no entity can
be considered in isolation. The entire universe is a
system in which no entity is an abstraction.10 Both
neo-mechanism and emergence argued for a single
process in the universe that is reflected in finite
conscious minds. This concept makes reality a whole
without the necessity of introducing ideas or categories. Such a position Whitehead sees as also compat-
ible with physics.

            In other words, it belongs to the
            nature of a 'being' that it is a
            potential for every 'becoming'. This
            is the 'principle of relativity'.11

    In accepting becoming as the chief metaphysical
category, the activity of consciousness is seen to
reflect this principle by being a felt relationship; a

157

relationship between a subject and an object.12
Whitehead also admits the reality of objects, which do
not depend for their reality upon subjects. Such
objects may rightly be called 'eternal' as their
integrity is maintained before and after their unity
with the subject. Furthermore, Whitehead says that
all eternal objects are available to the subject, as
subjects and objects share the same characteristics of
being actual entities. He uses the term 'felt' to
describe the response of a subject to the 'ingression'
of an object. Alexander and Morgan tended to say that
a subject 'enjoyed' its objects. Nevertheless, the
principle involved is the same.

Whitehead also suggests that the resulting unity
of subject and object produces novelty.13 This point
he summarizes by saying, "'Change' is the description
of the adventures of eternal objects in the evolving
universe of actual things."14

According to Whitehead, the activity or process
of the universe -- becoming -- is the principle of
limitation for consciousness as a whole. Because of
its dipolar nature this principle allows for both unity
and diversity, and it participates in the process of
events. Its unity is the totality of relationships
that make up the actual world at any given instant.
Its diversity is the indeterminateness of feelings
which produce novel actuality.

Having outlined what the principle of limitation
is, we must next consider how Whitehead understood this
principle functioning for consciousness. In other
words, we must clarify that becoming is the same as
conscious activity. First we will analyze becoming
as the conscious activity of the cosmic entity --
God --, and second as the conscious activity of
finite conscious entities.

Universal conscious activity can be explained
metaphysically by the suggestion that God himself has
three natures: The 'primordial nature' by which God is
understood as a conceptual unity of all feelings

and all eternal objects; the 'consequent nature', by which God is understood as the unity of all physical prehensions in the evolving universe; and, the 'superjective nature', by which God is understood as receiving specific satisfaction from novelty.15

Throughout this book we have discussed that process must be composed of interrelations of unity and diversity, which form a self-perpetuating system. The unity and diversity in their purest forms make up the primordial nature of God. This diversity Whitehead calls eternal objects, and the unity is God's conceptual analysis of all these objects as a unity. On the level of pure potentials eternal objects can only be understood as potentials for the process of becoming.16

The primordial unity is God's conceptual prehension of all eternal objects and feelings as a unity. Such a conception is a 'mental' reality; thus the primordial unity is also called the 'mental pole'.17 One can likewise speak of the multiplicity of eternal objects as the 'physical pole'. The mental pole functions as a plan; it is the plan that the multiplicity shall form a complex unity.

The multiplicity as pure potential and the mental pole as a conceptual plan have no specific physical content. This content must be supplied during the actual process by which eternal objects form complex unities. The outcomes of this process is God's 'consequent nature'. Nevertheless, in both of these two natures, God remains essentially the same. That is God is everlastingly a unity of all multiplicity.

Of course the question can be raised as to why there is a process at all, if God is everlastingly the same. The answer to this depends upon God's third nature -- the 'superjective nature'. God allows process because he enjoys the novelty resulting from the process. God has feelings. Each bit of novelty, which brings the universe toward a greater unity, results in a satisfaction for God. It is this third nature that gives the reason for acting at all.

Thus for the universal consciousness, the unity of becoming is an abstract conception of the total unity of all relationships. The concrete content of this unity is the totality of relationships in the actual world. This is not the first time that a thinker has conceived of unity as having an abstract and a concrete aspect in consciousness. On the other hand, for Whitehead, diversity also has two aspects. Its abstract aspect is the pure potential of the eternal objects, and its concrete aspect is the novelty of new relationships in the external world. Here a new concept is introduced into Process thought. Diversity like unity is given an abstract content of its own in terms of eternal objects. In other words, diversity is not merely a division of some primordial unity, but is itself equally primordial. Alexander's suggestion of Space-Time dividing itself would not be consistent with Whitehead's point. As we will recall, the principle of limitation participated in the process of events for Alexander and Varisco by first dividing itself. Whitehead now suggests that the principle of limitation applies to the universal consciousness, rather than being a universal consciousness.

Having noted this new element introduced by Whitehead, we will now consider the second part of our stated purpose by seeing how the activity of finite consciousnesses is the same as becoming. Whitehead says. "Every actual entity has the capacity for knowledge; but, in general, knowledge seems to be negligible apart from a peculiar complicity in the constitution of some mental occasion."18 The word 'consciousness' Whitehead prefers to reserve for those actual entities in which knowledge is primary rather than negligible.19 Thus instead of saying that consciousness is a characteristic of all reality, he speaks of feeling as that characteristic. "In place of the Hegelian hierarchy of categories of thought, the philosophy of organism finds a hierarchy of categories of feeling.'20

Consciousness arises on the level of feelings when an actual entity as subject forms a proposition concerning its object -- when propositions become a part of feeling. A proposition is a judgment about the future, potential meaning of an object to a subject. In other words, on the level of consciousness, subjects not only receive data from the eternal objects composing their object, but the subject also makes judgments about those objects. The forming of propositions leads to the necessity of making further judgments. These judgments may prove to be valid or in error. In either case, the judgments create a novel situation -- one that could not have been predicted.

There is another metaphysical implication associated with the formulation of judgments. Judgments imply a theory of 'probability'.21 The question is to understand the way in which probability arises. It arises first, because the subject has learned in previous experience that all actual occasions arise out of a particular environment. Second, the particular elements involved in a given actual occasion have been abstracted from that environment. Third, to make a judgment about these elements is also to say something about the environment. And fourth, since in the future elements will continue to exist in a very similar environment, one has grounds for judging with high probability the future position of those elements in their environment.22

In other words probability arises from the fact that reality is a single process. Reality has novelty, but it is not chaotic.

Still another implication, associated with the formation of judgments, is that they assume a unity of all reality. That is, a judgment is based on the conceptual 'ideal' of a total unity within the experience of a certain level of complex unity. In one sense a judgment is based on a vision -- it is religious. Whitehead says, regarding this topic: "Religion is the vision of something which stands beyond, behind, and within, the passing flux of

immediate things; something which is real, and yet wait-
ing to be realized; something which is a remote
possibility, and yet the greatest of present facts;
something that gives meaning to all that passes, and
yet eludes apprehension; something whose possession is
the final goal, and yet is beyond all reach; something which is the ultimate ideal, and the hopeless
quest."23

The level of judgments is the level of feeling
which has God as a felt object; God being understood
as the complex unity of all things. Above the electron
the only level of emergence significant to Whitehead is
the emergence of the mental pole -- the conceptual
unity of feelings and eternal objects. The feelings on
the level of a mental pole are also called 'intellectual feelings'.25

Such intellectual feelings are normally believed
to exist only in humans. However, Whitehead points out
that we have no means of testing this assumption in
any crucial way.26 Therefore, while consciousness may
be, as panpsychism tends to think, an element of all
reality, this statement cannot be critically validated,
and it is not to be applied metaphysically.

For finite consciousness, as for the cosmic
consciousness, activity requires both unity and
diversity. Moreover, for finite consciousnesses as
for the cosmic consciousness, both unity and diversity
have a concrete and an abstract aspect. The concrete
aspect of diversity for finite consciousnesses is the
object of consciousness, and the abstract aspect is a
judgment about the object based on probability. The
concrete aspect of unity for finite consciousnesses is
the present knowledge of the subject, and the abstract
aspect is an 'ideal' of a total unity having God as its
felt object. Thus we may conclude that the principle
of limitation functions the same for the finite
consciousnesses and for the cosmic consciousness.

As limitation for Whitehead had two aspects, it is
not adequate to say, along with the pre-Whiteheadians,

162

that its abstract aspect is only that of an 'ideal'
total unity. As we may recall, the term absolute is
usually applied by Process thinkers to the abstract
aspect of unity, which in turn is the full abstract
aspect of limitation. Interestingly, Whitehad himself
uses the term absolute to refer to the abstract aspect
of unity, but, as we have seen, for Whitehead, unity
does not exhaust limitation; diversity also has an
abstract aspect. This point requires further investigation. In order to make this investigation we must
consider Whitehead's concept of 'Creativity'.

According to Whitehead all entities contain the
principle of 'creativity'. For example he says,

> God is in the world, or nowhwere,
> creating continually in us and
> around us. This creative principle
> is everywhere, in animate and so-
> called inanimate matter, in the
> ether, water, earth, human hearts.
> But this creation is a continuing
> process and 'the process itself is
> the actuality', since no sooner do
> you arrive than you start on a
> fresh journey. In so far as man
> partakes of the divine, of God,
> and that participation is his
> immortality, reducing the question
> of whether his individuality sur-
> vives death of the body to an
> irrelevancy. His true dignity as
> co-creator in the universe is his
> dignity and his grandure.27

At first the above may appear unclear or con-
fused. On the one hand we are told that to participate
in the creative process is to 'partake of the divine'.
On the other hand Whitehead calls man a 'co-creator in
the universe'. If God and creativity are rightly
equated, it makes some sense to say that to partake
of the process is to partake of God. Such a position
would surely imply that ultimately God alone is the

creator; thus making the statement that man is the co-creator rather unintelligible.

Looked at from the other side, if man is a co-creator, one must assume that he partakes of creativity in his own right. Furthermore, if he partakes of creativity in his own right, it would make rather good sense to say that creativity must be a metaphysical principle in which all entities, including God, participate; but each of these entities including God is subordinate to or not inclusive of creativity. If all entities contain the principle of creativity, and if no entity, including God, totally incorporates this principle, then it might seem that creativity is an abstract idea of that which unifies all reality.

A concept, such as process or the principle of creativity, according to Whitehead, requires a physical object.28 In ADVENTURES OF IDEAS he says, "All knowledge is conscious discrimination of objects experienced."29

As we said earlier, knowing is a process of inter-action between subject and object. A significant aspect of knowing an object is a process of limitation, whereby the subject's and object's particular interests and values emphasize only certain relations while push-ing others into the background; making knowing possible. In a relative universe, in which everything participates in every other thing, a principle of limi-tation is always needed to make knowledge possible.

We may well be prepared to accept these two con-cepts concerning the possibility of knowledge, namely: (1) that all knowledge depends upon an object, or that physical feelings always come before conceptual feel-ings; and, (2) that knowledge of an object is possible in a relative universe only by a principle of limita-tion. Before accepting these premises we must be reminded that both presuppose our knowledge about knowledge, and our knowledge of a principle of limitation. In other words, we must answer the ques-tions; What is the object of our concept of knowledge?

164

and, What is the object of our concept of the principle of limitation? To these questions Whitehead answers, God.

> If we reject this alternative behind the scenes, we must provide a ground for limitation which stands among the attributes of the substantial activity. This attribute provides the limitation for which no reason can be given; for all reason flows from it. God is the ultimate limitation, and His existence is the ultimate irrationality. For no reason can be given for just that limitation which stands in His nature to impose. God is not concrete, but He is the ground for concrete actuality. No reason can be given for the nature of God, because that nature is the ground of rationality.30

God is the ultimate limit of reason, because he is the objectification of the ultimate principle of creativity. He is the object of our concept of how rationality is possible. Furthermore, he is the limit to which all concrete reference is made. Whitehead also says that God or Deity provides such factors as importance, value and ideal reality. These factors allow man to formulate the concept of a transcendent universe. In other words, God gives us a concept of unity, but it is a unity of realized actualities.31 God reveals to us creativity as infinite possibilities, but makes such a concept available by also limiting the infinity of possibilities to those already realized in some way.32

At this point it is clearly possible to re-introduce a specific reference to the term absolute. The term absolute refers to the particular unity of realized possibilities objectified as the absolute pole of God. This is how we have explained the reference of the term absolute many times in our discussions of Process. It is a unity of a given present, which serves as the necessary object of physical feelings and a principle of limitation, and which allows for our knowledge of the totally undetermined unity of the principle of creativity. God is the objectification of creativity in the double sense of being an object for physical feelings and a principle of limitation. The two poles of God, the absolute and the relative, are the objectification of the ultimate categories of 'many' and 'one'. 33

The absolute pole must necessarily be understood as a particular unity. It is the unity of all realized possibilities, i.e., the unity of the past of the cosmos. Of course, even understood as a particular unity the absolute pole may be rightly called abstract. As it stands at the very limits of man's reason, it may be only a vague background feeling.34 On the other hand, as we have already mentioned, the absolute pole is a particular unity because it is the objectification of the ultimate category of the 'one'; which is an aspect of the principle of creativity. To apply the term absolute to creativity, or to God equated with creativity, i.e., creativity subjectively, is to suggest that ultimately there is one particular unity.

The implications of such a suggestion were introduced before. In summary, such a suggestion implies that the process of the universe culminates in the realization of a particular predetermined unity. God, one might say, becomes an absolute unity as the multiplicity of the relative pole is more and more taken into the absolute pole. In which case, the absolute pole is understood as the ultimate determination of the process within the universe.

The above is further clarified if we look again at Whitehead's concept of God. According to Whitehead God is an actual entity. In expanding this idea he says,

> Thus, analogously to all entities,
> the nature of God is dipolar...
> One side of God's nature is constituted

by his conceptual experience. This
experience is the primordial fact
in the world, limited by no actuality which it presupposes. It
is therefore infinite, devoid of
all negative prehension. This side of
his nature is free, complete,
primordial, eternal, actually
deficient and unconscious. The other
side originates with physical experience derived from the temporal
world, and then acquires integration
with the primordial side. It is
determined, incomplete, consequent,
'everlasting', fully actual, and
conscious. His necessary goodness
expresses the determination of his
consequent nature.35

The issue to which the above addresses itself is
how God is to be understood as an actual entity, who
is the objectification of creativity for all other
actual entities. The answer is that for God unity, or
the conceptual pole, does not require an object. God
as the objectification of creativity is the primordial
embodiment of the conceptual. God's pole of unity is
described as 'free, complete, primordial, eternal,'
because it depends upon no particular unity. The unity
primordial to God is of the character of the unity of
creativity -- undetermined.

Relative to the events which originate in the
temporal world, God's conceptual pole becomes a particular unity. This particular unity is described as
'determined, incomplete, consequent,' etc. To this
particular unity the term absolute can be correctly
applied. It serves man as an object of his concept
of unity. However, as God requires no object for his
conceptual pole, continuing change, which from the
human viewpoint contradicts the term absolute -- referring to a particular unity -- does not in fact alter
God's primordial nature. Indeed, the unity of whatever
events originate in the temporal world correctly

167

express the primordially, undetermined nature of unity. God, we might say, is the Subject by virtue of his conceptual pole. That is, he is creativity objecti- fied. He is Object for the world, because by a scheme of limitation his particular unity can serve as a physical feeling, which gives rise to a conceptual feeling of the principle of the indeterminate 'one'.36

What emerges from our study of Whitehead is that his understanding of the absolute pole is chiefly a temporal concept. The absolute pole is the unity of the past of consciousness held in the divine. The absolute pole is the unity of the history of reality. The past of the divine consciousness is also the whole of the pasts of all finite consciousnesses.

As we have seen, the past does serve as a prin- ciple of limitation. The past of any consciousness limits its own present possibilities. We discussed earlier the problem that Whitehead's epistemology did not explain how the pasts of finite consciounesses were unified. Now we have the answer in the concept of God's absolute pole.

Of course, the absolute pole of God is not the only factor which unifies reality. As Whitehead said, all entities are a part of the creative advance. The absolute pole gives a unity of 'mutual immediacy'. In other words, the whole of the past limits the mutual present of all entities, just as the past of a single entity limits its present possibilities.

Unless the principle of limitation participates in the process of events it is deterministic. Clearly the past does participate in the process of events. Earlier we saw Whitehead point out that past experience is an essential factor in the ability of finite consci- ousness to make judgments about the future meaning of its objects. Without the past being durationally present, finite consciousness has no future aim. Likewise, on the cosmic level, the absolute pole is necessary for God's subjective aim. Without God's aim there would be no cosmic future. The participation of the past in the establishment of the future, which in turn becomes the past, demonstrates that the principle of limitation participates in the process of events.

Whitehead suggested that the past of a finite consciousness must be joined with the presentational immediacy of the felt objects before judgments can be formed. This understanding of the absolute pole does not allow it to divide itself into the diversity of objects necessary for consciousness. While Whitehead's absolute pole does participate in the process of events it does not do so by dividing itself. At this point Whitehead differs from several other Process thinkers.

Diversity, which is one part of the primordial potential for activity, is a necessary aspect for the divine consciousness as it is for finite consciousnesses. Of course, the divine consciousness differs from finite consciousnesses in that it can utilize the pure potential of eternal objects. Finite consciousnesses require events in which eternal objects adhere in a definite past of some actual entity. Indeed, as we saw, God could not be the object for finite consciousness without the absolute pole, which is the past.

The above formulation solves the great problem for Process thought concerning the understanding of the concept absolute. If, as the pre-Whiteheadians had said, one takes the term absolute as referring to some ultimate principle which dividies itself in order to produce diversity, then it is very difficult to consistently adopt the analogy of a conscious organism to describe the universe. The reason being that the consciousness of an organism requires that it have external objects. Yet if the absolute principle divides itself, the division must remain internal; otherwise, there would be no way of accounting for cosmic unity.

Whitehead suggests that the term absolute should not be applied to the whole of the cosmic consciousness, but merely to part of it. External to the unity, i.e., absolute pole, of the cosmic unity are the eternal objects. This dipolar nature of the cosmic consciousness is a primordial fact and not the result of a division of a primordial unity.

Here we must remind ourselves that, for Whitehead, the objects of finite consciousness are also called feelings. The fact that feelings are both external and also internal is what makes the interaction between subject and object possible. Furthermore, as we have seen, an object that becomes an internal feeling both remains the same and it also changes. It remains the same in that the eternal objects which compose it remain changeless. On the other hand, objects are changed by the subject's judgments about them based on the subject's particular past.

Likewise, the objects of the divine consciousness, when they become internal feelings, both remain the same in terms of eternal objects, but they are changed according to the unique past of God. While God's past is called the absolute pole, this usage of the term absolute does not logically preclude objects being external to the absolute pole.

For consciousness to occur in a finite organism, that organism must be a unity, dipolar in nature, and relative to its objects. By Whitehead's formulation, the divine consciousness is a unity, dipolar in nature, and relative to its objects. We conclude, therefore, that Whitehead has an understanding of process which is consistent on both a metaphysical and epistemological level. He has established an exact analogy between the activity of finite consciousness and the universal activity.

Nevertheless, this does not end the implications of the Whiteheadian system. According to Whitehead reality is unified in two ways. First it is unified by the fact that all entities share a common principle of creativity. Seacond reality is unified by a common past retained in the absolute pole of God. Both aspects of unity have an essential impact on conscious activity, and neither denies diversity. The former is the source of pure potential. As Whitehead says, "This factor of activity is what I have called 'Creativity'."[37] The potential is made available to finite actual entities only through the actual entity God. Without God there would be no principle of limitation for consciousness.

Creativity itself offers an infinity of possibilities for activity. However, as we have seen in our consideration, finite consciousness cannot function apart from some limitation of possibilities. The absolute pole of God is the only one of the two forms of unity that can serve consciousness as a principle of limitation, because the absolute pole, being the concrete unity of the past, limits the present of any actual entity to a finite number of possibilities, and thus provides an 'aim' for that entity.

Moreover, the fact that at present the number of possibilities for any finite entity are limited by the absolute pole does not mean that an infinite number of possibilities cannot also exist. Because of the principle of creativity the potential possibilities open to the universe as a whole are infinite. Another way of describing the infinity of possibilities for the universe is by pointing out that the particular possibilities that are now realized were not predetermined to be realized.

God, from his unique perspective, may judge with the greatest possible accuracy the probability of future events. After all, with the whole of the past for reference, God knows better than any other entity the probable future. Nevertheless, even God participates in creativity, which is ultimately an indeterminate activity.

The distinction which Whitehead maintains between God and the principle of creativity leads to the final conclusion that all actual entities share in the creative process. It is this idea in particular that attracted the attention of several theologians who

171

became followers of Whiteheadian thought. Indeed is was theology, along with philosophy, that carried Process thought from Whitehead to the present. The next stage in the history of Process thought, must be read and understood to include the works of Process theologians.

1 Whitehead, Alfred North. SYMBOLISM ITS MEANING AND EFFECT. (Cambridge: University Press, 1928). pp. 11-12.
2 ibid. pp. 17-19.   3 p. 27.   4 p. 41.
5 p. 58.   6 p. 59.   7 p. 66.
8 Whitehead. MODES OF THOUGHT. p. 223.
9 Whitehead, Alfred North. PROCESS AND REALITY. (Cambridge: University Press, 1929). p. vii.
10 ibid. p. 3.   11 p. 30.   12 p. 56.
13 p. 62.   14 p. 81.   15 pp. 121-122.
16 p. 208.   17 p. 122.   18 p. 225.
19 p. 227.   20 p. 232.
21 pp. 288-289.   22 pp. 292-293.
23 Whitehead, Alfred North. SCIENCE AND THE MODERN WORLD. (Cambridge: University Press, 1925). pp. 267-268.
24 Whitehead. PROCESS AND REALITY. p. 349.
25 ibid. p. 386.   26 p. 390.
27 DIALOGUES OF ALFRED NORTH WHITEHEAD. recorded by Lucien Prince. (London: Max Reinhart, 1954). p. 366.
28 PROCESS AND REALITY. p. 349.
29 ADVENTURES OF IDEAS. p. 227
30 SCIENCE AND THE MODERN WORLD. pp. 249-250.
31 MODES OF THOUGHT. p. 140.
32 PROCESS AND REALITY. p. 229.
33 ADVENTURES OF IDEAS. p. 241.   34 ibid. p. 18.
35 PROCESS AND REALITY. p. 488.   36 ibid. p. 489.
37 ADVENTURES OF IDEAS. p. 230.

CHAPTER XVIII

FOUNDATIONS OF PROCESS THEOLOGY

The distinction which Whitehead maintains between God and the principle of creativity is a problem for Christian theological tradition, because that tradition has made God the sole Creator. It would have been more consistent with the tradition if Whitehead had called God the creative principle, and sole unifying force in the universe. As it is, creativity appears to become a god beyond God. However, to equate Whitehead's dipolar God with creativity requires that one accept a deterministic system, and give up the analogy between a conscious organism and the universal activity; and the dipolar concept of the universe. These points require more explanation.

If one accepts the dipolar God as a conscious actual entity unique because of his universal perspective, then the divine consciousness like finite consciousnesses must have a principle of limitation. If a dipolar God and the ultimate principle of activity, i.e., creativity, are one, then the only possible limit for divine consciousness would be an ultimate concrete unity of all reality. Indeed, equating a dipolar God with creativity would mean that the term absolute refers to a concrete unity of all reality within God. Such an understanding of an ultimate concrete unity, as we have seen, implies that activity of the universe moves toward a final goal -- a total unity. When the whole of reality is taken up into a concrete unity, then the Whiteheadian concept of dipolarity must be set aside. Equating a dipolar God with creativity cannot satisfy the Whiteheadian cosmology.

Of course, some objective idealisms, for example, attempt to maintain that God is conscious and yet not dipolar in the Whiteheadian sense. However, we have presented conclusive evidence against the possibility of activity being explained in this way.

Another alternative was the suggestion that the analogy between a conscious organism and the universal activity cannot be maintained. In this case one may either deny that activity is organized at all, or else choose something like mechanism, which says that activity is ordered by an abstract physical principle.

We have already explained why Process cannot accept traditional objective idealism or mechanism. Therefore, in order to consistently avoid determinism, while retaining the Process model for consciousness, Whitehead must not associate the concept of absoluteness with the ultimate principle of activity. At the same time he must retain the concept 'absolute pole' as a principle of limitation for conscious activity. Both of these he accomplished by drawing a distinction between the unity of the single conscious entity God, and the principle of unity in creativity, which all entities share.

What this distinction suggests is that, while conscious unity depends upon God as conscious, unity qua unity does not. Likewise, while conscious unity requires a principle of limitation, in the form of God's absolute pole, unity of itself has no concrete limits. Nevertheless, we must not suppose that conscious activity is essentially different from the principle of creativity. Indeed the very existence of consciousness proves its participation in creativity. Another way of stating this point is to say that while the activity of our particular universe follows the model of consciousness, we cannot suppose that another universe, in another epoch, might not follow a different model. Although we must add that activity would always be composed of unity and diversity.1

While maintaining the concept of God's absolute pole and relative pole, Whitehead could not equate God with creativity. As we have seen, the term absolute must refer to both a particular concrete content and to a principle of limitation. Creativity, on the other hand, has no particular concrete content, and is unlimited activity. Nevertheless, it is

possible to read some of Whitehead's major works in
such a way that the term absolute would appear to
apply to creativity. For example, in PROCESS AND
REALITY 'creativity' is one of the three members of
the 'Category of Ultimates' along with 'many' and
'one'.2 Furthermore, as John Cobb points out in A
CHRISTIAN NATURAL THEOLOGY, Whitehead's use of the
concept of creativity changes in the history of his
writings:

> In Science And The Modern World, we
> encounter four metaphysical principles:
> the underlying substantial activity
> and its three attributes -- eternal
> objects, actual entities, and the
> principle of limitation. In
> Religion in The Making, subtle but
> important changes have occurred in
> the understanding of these four
> elements in the philosophic system...
> Since God is now considered as an
> actual entity, we might consider
> the four metaphysical principles
> reduced to three: creativity, eternal
> objects, and actual entities includ-
> ing God as a special case.3

Cobb concludes his very important analysis of the
history of the development of the concept of creativity
in Whitehead by saying: "Clearly he retained throughout
his life the sense that the ultimate fact is the
process itself of which God, the eternal objects, and
the temporal occasions are all explanatory."4

A dilemma for theology, growing out of the idea
that Whitehead used the term absolute to refer to
creativity as "Absolute" is already clear. If
creativity is really called absolute -- in the usual
sense of that term --, then a distinction between it
and God subordinates God to creativity in all of his
aspects. In which case, creativity becomes a 'god'
beyond God. It is this very concern which drove
Bishop Temple to say,

175

...if only Professor Whitehead would
for creativity say Father, for
'primordial nature of God' say
Eternal Word, and for the 'consequent nature of God' say Holy Spirit,
he would perhaps be able to show
ground for his gratifying conclusions.
But he cannot use those terms,
precisely because each of them
imports the notion of Personality
as distinct from Organism. The
very reason which gives to the
Christian scheme its philosophic
superiority is that what precludes
Professor Whitehead from adopting
it.5

The solution to the above theological problem,
taken by Lionel Thornton, was to equate God with the
ultimate activity. "God", he says, "is thus Absolute
Activity, not in process of realization but in concrete
unchangeable reality."6 As we will see later, this
solution poses considerable problems in relation to
several important Whiteheadian concepts. In particular, we will see that this solution necessarily leads
to the denial of God's dipolar nature. Furthermore,
Thornton's move is unnecessary, because God's
absoluteness does not depend upon his being equated
with creativity. As we have seen, creativity for
Whitehead does not have the attribute of absoluteness.

One possible theological alternative to
Thornton's solution is to find some way to understand
the term absolute as referring to a pole of God,
while avoiding the conclusion that creativity is a god
beyond God. Charles Hartshorne, along with his other
contributions to Process, addressed this key question
of the relation between God and creativity. He, like
Whitehead, is a philosopher rather than a theologian.
Nevertheless, many of his writings are on the
philosophy of religion; making Hartshorne a connecting
link between Whitehead and a large number of the
Process theologians. In general Hartshorne's work

represents an attempt to understand the term absolute as referring to one pole of God, along with a relative pole. Unlike Thornton, he does not attempt to make creativity or activity the Absolute.

Hartshorne's willingness to adopt the Process understanding of absoluteness comes in part from the fact that he sees it validating the view of God held by most theologians and religious people; namely, "The 'strand' which theologians on the whole, still propose to retain, and which is alone self-consistent, as judged by its relations to the other strand, is the popularly familiar definition of God as everlasting, all-controlling, all-knowing, and ethically-good or 'holy' to the highest possible degree."7

Process, he feels, can validate this view against the long standing dogmatic position, which, he will show, is, in view of Process, filled with contradictions. The dogmatic or 'secular-strand', based on Greek thought rather than Christian experience, he illustrates as follows:

> God, for all the church writers, and
> for many others, including Spinoza,
> was the 'absolutely infinite', the
> altogether maximal, supreme, or
> perfect, being. All his properties,
> including the popular religious ones
> so far as philosophically valid, were
> to be deduced from this absoluteness
> or perfection, as is so beautifully
> explained by St, Thomas Aquinas.8

Some of the implications of this secular view Hartshorne sums up: "It simply denies certain all-pervasive, infinitely fundamental aspects of life -- change, variety, complexity, receptivity, sympathy, suffering, memory, anticipation -- as relevant to the idea of God."9 Furthermore, he says that this brand of theism implies that "no act can, in its consequences, be better than any other,"10 as God in himself remains impassible to all human actions.

Finally, he says that this type of theism makes complete nonsense out of the Incarnation. If, as he says, Jesus is really suppose to be God loving man, it is quite contradictory to suggest that God is absent from all events in the temporal world.11

The above criticisms result in large part from the dogmatic application of the Greek view of absoluteness. By adopting the Process usage of the term absolute, Hartshorne gives us quite different possibilities upon which to base a systematic theology. The point that we want to notice most carefully is that he sees God's absolute pole as not equated with an ultimate or supreme unity. He says, "On the other hand, if supreme is identical with absolute or non-relative, and yet the supreme includes all things, hence all relations, the result is a contradiction."12 Using this point, he does, as we might expect, adopt the position that the absolute pole is one aspect of God.

> I am arguing that the absolute is, rather, an abstract feature of the inclusive and supreme reality which is precisely the personal God. If one must speak of 'appearance', then the absolute, simply as such, may be termed the appearance of ultimate reality to the abstract cognition, including the divine self-cognition in its abstract aspect. The absolute is not more, but less, than God -- in the obvious sense in which the abstract is less than the concrete.13

The above quotation seems to be consistent with our interpretation of creativity as being distinct from God in Whiteheadian thought. First of all, here and in Whitehead, the term absolute refers to only an aspect of God, and not to something that is more than God, e.g., it does not refer to creativity. Second, here and in Whitehead, the absolute pole, as an aspect of the objectified God, makes possible human knowledge of God's own 'self-cognition in its abstract aspect,' i.e, the totally indeterminate unity of creativity. Indeed, Hartshorne later says, "We are an absolutely inessential (but not inconsequential) object for him; he is the essential object for us."14

Furthermore, like Whitehead, Hartshorne argues that the absolute pole is the pole of unity of relations, and that no relations fall outside of this pole.15 Consistent with Whiteheadian thought, the absolute pole is a unity of all realized relations. It serves as an object for man. There is no god beyond God, because all realized relations are unified in God's absolute pole. The potential for relations is possible between entities, because all entities, including God, share in creativity.

Having established that Hartshorne adopted the general Whiteheadian understanding of the term absolute, we may next consider how this influenced his philosophical contributions to theological thought. In the first place, his understanding lead to a re-evaluation of Anselm's ontological argument for the existence of God. What he saw in Anselm's argument is summarized in the following:

> What Anselm had discovered, or almost discovered, was that existence and actuality (or concreteness) are in principle distinct, and that two kinds of individuals may be conceived, those whose existence and actuality, although distinct, are both contingent and those -- or that one -- whose actuality but not existence is contingent, this second kind being superior to all others. According to this view, any individual, no matter how superior, exists by virtue of contingent concrete states; but whereas with you or me it is always possible that there should be no such states at all, with God, though any such state is contingent, that there is some such state is necessary.16

In studying the absolute pole as a principle of
limitation, we said that while man needed a particular
unity -- an object -- in order to conceptualize unity,
God was primordially a unity in one aspect, quite apart
from any object. Naturally, we were assuming in that
discussion that just as creativity included a multiplicity as well as a unity, so God, as creativity
objectified, included a relative as well as an absolute
pole. This meant that the pole of unity was necessarily made up of relations, but the particularity of
these relations was a concrete absolute unity only for
man. Picking up this point and developing it,
Hartshorne concludes that his formulation can be read
to mean that God depends upon no specific relations
for his existence, but only his actuality is contingent. On the other hand, man depends for both his
existence and his actuality on a particular state, just
as he depends upon a particular concrete aspect of the
absolute pole. Furthermore, as man depends for his
knowledge on an object, Whitehead said that, without a
particular actual unity, we could have no concept of
unity. Hartshorne goes on to say that to be able to
know God depends upon God's existence.17

The concrete aspect of the absolute pole is here
thought of as being a unity of all presently realized
relationships, and not a factor of total determination.
This means that relations themselves are not always
causally derived. "In final metaphysical analysis;
that acts occur for which there is no complete causal
derivation is not 'irrational' if the essential function of reason is to explicate and serve creativity
(rather than to foresee its results); deity, however,
cannot be conceived as a mere product of creativity,
but only as its supreme and indispensable aspect, whose
felxibility is coincident with possibility itself, and
is thus on both sides of every contingent alternative,
hence itself not contingent but necessary."18

A second reason to quote the above is to show
that, along with Whitehead, Hartshorne understands the
limits of conscious activity to be directly connected
with the concept of the absolute pole. The absolute

pole as an object makes it possible for us to conceptualize an indeterminate unity, i.e., the unity of
creativity itself. We are free because the principle
of unity is indeterminate. The absolute pole is a
particular unity in God, but it is accompanied by a
relative pole. God is contingent because the absolute
pole does form a unity of the past events of the
temporal world.19

It becomes quite clear that this formulation would
indeed make concepts such as change, variety, complexity, and sympathy relevant to our idea of God.
Furthermore, it gives a basis for the evaluation of
human actions. Those actions which are creative --
which promote new relations -- are of value.
Hartshorne expresses it this way: Man's purpose is to
be altruistic toward God, i.e., "to serve and glorify
God so as to contribute some value to the divine life
which at present it otherwise would not have."20
The point is expanded in the following:

> ...The exceptional status of God can
> itself be put as a transcendental or
> strictly universal rule. Thus "Every
> individual whatsoever interacts (at
> least) with some other individuals, and
> also, and in all possible cases, with
> God, who alone universally interacts.'
> This rule is absolute. For since God,
> in a fashion, interacts with, that is,
> both influences and (in subsequent
> state) is influenced by, himself, all
> individuals whatever interact with deity
> as well as with at least some individuals
> other than deity.21

Having shown that Hartshorne does adopt the
Whiteheadian position that the term absolute refers to
one pole of God, we then moved to a consideration of
how this understanding of the term absolute influenced
Hartshorne's general formulations about the existence
of God and his nature. Now we are ready to look at
certain further implications of these formulations

that are especially relevant to the development of a
Process theology. We shall consider in order the
topics of Christology, soteriology and eschatology.

The matter of Christology has already arisen in
Hartshorne's list of contradictions that result from
the traditional dogmatic view of God's absoluteness.
In particular Jesus is supposed to be a gift of God's
love toward men. This gift establishes a new relationship between God and man. But -- if God does not
engage in relationships, the conception is inconsistent.
As we have seen, the idea of God is constructed by
Hartshorne in such a way that absoluteness does not
prevent direct relationships between man and God. And
it is the directness of relationships that allows for
the possibility of manifestations of love.

On the other hand, Hartshorne's position presents
a Christological problem:

> Although I believe the doctrine of
> the Incarnation enshrined important
> religious truth, I fell in honesty
> bound to add the following. I very
> much doubt if there ever has been or
> ever can be a form of theism which
> will enable such phrases as 'Jesus
> was God' or the 'divinity of Jesus'
> to have a sufficiently unambiguous
> meaning to entitle them to serve as
> requirements for Christian unity.22

It is not difficult to understand the important
religious 'truth' which he means; namely, as he said
in another place, Jesus, if he has any meaning at all,
must be an example of God's love for men, i.e., God's
relatedness to man. Notice that he did not refer to
Jesus as the example or revelation of God's love.23
Such a stand would be impossible from the Process
viewpoint, partly because of its special understanding
of the term absolute. God as absolute, in the traditional sense, cannot relate directly to man. By the
Process view, the absolute pole, which is nothing other

182

than the particular unity of relationships between
God and the world, is itself the objectification of
God's participation with man that Jesus is supposed
to reveal. In other words, we know God by our own
participation in creating with God.24 God's relation
to man is not to be understood in terms of a single
event such as the Incarnation; rather God relates to
man through all events.

Hartshorne does admit that individuals may be
gifted in special ways. It is possible that Jesus
was such a gifted individual. He may have manifested
divine love in some special sense.25 Of course this
is hardly a typical view of Jesus. In fact the
problem of how Jesus can represent a unique relationship between God and the world, which results in part
from the understanding of the term absolute, will
regularly reoccur in our study.

The point at which we will take up soteriology is
with a consideration of the common Christian analogy
of participation in the 'Body of Christ', as a
description of the salvific state. To begin with,
St.Paul refers to Jesus as the head of the body. Such
an organic-social analogy is open to at least two very
different interpretations, called by Henri Bergson
'closed' and 'opened' understandings of society.
Bergson says, "...if we wish to deal with fully
complete societies, clear-cut organizations of distinct
individuals, we must take the two perfect types of
association represented by a society of insects and
a human society, the one immutable, the other subject
to change; the one instinctive, the other intelligent;
the first similar to an organism whose elements exist
only in the interest of the whole, the second leaving
so wide a margin to the individual that we cannot tell
whether the organism was made for them or they for the
organism."26

In large part the interpretation of an organic-
social analogy that one chooses depends upon his
understanding of the concept of absoluteness. According to Karl Popper, if one adopts the Platonic under-

standing of God's absoluteness, a closed society
results from the interpretation.27   Popper points out
that for Plato forms, including the form of the Good,
are changeless. Change can only be away from the
forms.28 Man can change only for the worse, i.e.,
decay. Only reason can break the law of decay by allowing man to return to the forms.29 Following the
Platonic concepts, to become part of the 'Body of
Christ' is to return to a divinely predetermined plan.
It is to become a part of a society with a single
purpose as determined by Christ, its head.

Popper's argument seems conclusive on the point
that the Greek interpretation of absoluteness makes
salvation a conformity to a predetermined plan. It is
the sacrificing of one's individuality for the common
good of the whole. The rejection of individualism
Popper traces to "Plato's identification of individualism with egoism (which) furnishes him with a powerful weapon for his defense of collectivism as well as
for his attack upon individualism."30 As we move
ahead it will become clear that the 'Body of Christ'
analogy often falls under the influence of the Greek
understanding of absoluteness.

Certainly Process is interested in finding an
analogy to describe relations. But relations cannot be
established on the basis of man coming into line with
a predetermined plan of unity. Granted Process does
think of the absolute pole as a unity of relationships;
Process' absolute pole as a unity is not ultimately a
particular unity. Thus the very useful organic-social
analogy must take on a different emphasis for Process.

In sum, then, God's volition is
related to the world as though
every object in it were to him a
nerve-muscle, and his omiscience
is related to it as though every
object were a muscle-nerve. A
brain cell is for us, as it were,
a nerve-muscle, and a muscle-nerve,
in that its internal motions

184

respond to our thoughts, and our
thoughts to its motions. If there
is a theological analogy, here is
the locus. God has no separate
sense organs or muscles, because
all parts of the world body directly
perform both functions for him.
In this sense the world is God's
body.31

The above analogy clearly implies the necessity of
real individuality. The necessary unity is one for
individuals, and as such it is not a unity which makes
for a final and perfect harmony.32

If there is an ultimate concrete unity one may
think of evil as being overcome through perfect harmony.
On the other hand, if the absolute pole is merely a
unity of the various relationships growing out of the
temporal world; perfect harmony is a contradiction, and
in a strict sense evil cannot be overcome.

The understanding of the term absolute in Process
affects soteriological formulations in such a way that
the concept of the overcoming of evil by a perfect
harmony is inconsistent. This is certainly true in
the sense in which Jesus is thought to overcome evil.
According to Process the price of overcoming evil would
be to eliminate all possibilities; including possibilities for good.

In a strict sense of 'last things' one can hardly
speak of a Process eschatology. It is of course true
that Process is interested in the future. It looks to
the infinite possibilities that confront humanity as
a real hope. Whitehead himself says, "I wish I could
convey this sense I have of the infinity of the
possibilities that confront humanity -- the limitless
variation of choice, the possibility of novel and
untried combination, the happy turns of experiment, the
endless horizons opening out."33

Yet, influenced by an understanding of the term

absolute, this hope is not an eschatology. The new, as we know, is the result of new relations, which in turn form a part of the concrete content of God's absolute pole. Hartshorne points out, "It is true that there can be no absolutely maximal complexity; however, transcendence as such is not properly defined as an unsurpassable maximum of this or that."34

The absolute pole, being the objectification of a totally indeterminate unity, cannot be properly understood as a maximal complexity -- a certain predetermined level of relatedness. That would imply that there is a finite number of possible relationships, and that after these have been achieved the absolute pole is realized as a maximal complexity. While such a view would indeed allow the creation of an Absolute in time, it contradicts itself by the assumption of an absolute determination standing behind the absoluteness of temporal relations. This Whiteheadian Process, as we have seen, does not affirm. Yet some writers will attempt to make something like this the Process position.

Hartshorne's writings set the stage for the development of Process theology. He was a careful student of Whitehead's, who attempted at every point to remain as consistent as possible with Process. Of course he saw that Process had special implications for theology, and as a philosopher he tried to state them in a clear and concise way. He never tried to write a Process theology.

1 Whitehead. PROCESS AND REALITY. p. 28.
2 ibid. p. 28.
3 Cobb, John B., Jr. A CHRISTIAN NATURAL THEOLOGY.
      (London: Lutterworth Press, 1966). pp. 148-149.
4 ibid. p. 168.
5 Temple, William. NATURE MAN AND GOD. (London:
      Macmillan, 1934). p. 259.
6 Thornton, Lionel. THE INCARNATE LORD. (London:
      Longmans Green, 1928). p. 86.

7 Hartshorne, Charles. MAN'S VISION OF GOD. (Hamden, Connecticut: Archon Books, 1964). pp. 4-5.
8 ibid. p. 5   9 p. 125.
10 p. 156.   11 p. 168.
12 Hartshorne, Charles. THE DIVINE RELATIVITY. (New Haven: Yale University Press, 1948). p. 61.
13 ibid. p. 38.   14 pp. 141-142.
15 Hartshorne. MAN'S VISION OF GOD. pp. 238-239.
16 Hartshorne, Charles. ANSELM'S DISCOVERY. (LaSalle, Illinois: Open Court, 1965). p. 40.
17 ibid. p. 53.   18 p. 71.   19 p. 109.
20 Hartshorne. THE DIVINE RELATIVITY. p. 133.
21 Hartshorne, Charles. A NATURAL THEOLOGY FOR OUR TIME. (LaSalle, Illinois: Open Court, 1967). p.63.
22 Hartshorne, Charles. REALITY AS SOCIAL PROCESS. (Glencoe, Illinois: Free Press, 1953). p. 152.
23 Hartshorne. MAN'S VISION OF GOD. p. 165.
24 Hartshorne. ANSELM'S DISCOVERY. p. 51.
25 Hartshorne. REALITY AS SOCIAL PROCESS p. 153.
26 Bergson, Henri. THE TWO SOURCES OF MORALITY AND RELIGION. trans., R. Ashley Audra and Cloudesley Brereton. (New York: Doubleday). p. 117.
27 Popper, Karl R. THE OPEN SOCIETY AND ITS ENEMIES. (London: Routledge & Kegan Paul, 1952). Second Edition. Vol. I., p. 3.
28 ibid. p. 14   29 p. 20.   30 p. 101.
31 Hartshorne. MAN'S VISION OF GOD. p. 185.
32 ibid. p. 195.
33 DIALOGUES OF ALFRED NORTH WHITEHEAD. p. 169.
34 Hartshorne, Charles. CREATIVE SYNTHESIS AND THE PHILOSOPHIC METHOD. (London: SCM Press, 1970) p. 236.

CHAPTER XIX

WILLIAM CHRISTIAN'S
INFLUENCE ON THEOLOGY

William Christian, like Hartshorne, is better
called a philosopher than a theologian. However, his
book AN INTERPRETATION OF WHITEHEAD'S METAPHYSICS needs
to be considered, because it is a strong re-emphasis of
some of the Process influences on theology. In his
well known discussion of 'actual occasions' Christian
makes it quite clear that the 'absolute' in
Whiteheadian thought cannot be an ultimate concrete
unity of all reality. This, as the reader will recall,
was one of the chief considerations of Process thought
that attracted the attention of theologians. Specifically Christian says,

> The satisfaction of an actual
> occasion is an immediate feeling,
> which, when it perishes, exists as
> an object for occasions which
> succeed it... In its feeling of
> satisfaction the occasion has be-
> come a complete and fully concrete
> thing. If an occasion were only
> a process of internal change, it
> would not be complete or fully
> concrete.1

The point seems to be that an entity, or occasion,
cannot be fully concrete without its own unique aspect
of unity. The defense of this view is quite important
for our purposes. It suggests that if Process'
absolute pole is equated with the principle of unity,
then no entity other than God would have a concrete
unity of its own. The foregoing is the same as denying
that a true diversity exists among actual entities. A
distinction must be made between God's unity and a
unity shared by all entities individually.

Given the fact that there must be a real multiplicity in order to account for activity, the boundary

of each actual occasion must be defined. That is, each actual entity must have a unity of its own. Such definite boundaries may be accounted for scientifically by the thesis that no two actual occasions can have any spatiotemporal parts in common.2 If, as was suggested before, the absolute pole, as a particular unity, is part of an actual entity -- God -- then it could not include other actual occasions' spatiotemporal parts.

The absolute pole, understood as the ultimate principle of unity, suggests Christian, does not allow for individuality.3 Specifically Christian argues that the absolute pole, while itself a unity, does not provide unity for 'events'. It is a unity of objects and not of events. It is, so to speak, the Object of objects. It includes the sum total of the past.4

Furthermore, Christian believes that Whitehead intended to suggest just such a concept. "He thinks the 'underlying unity', which Bradley rightly asked for, does not have to be the Absolute."5 If the Absolute and the principle of unity are one in the same, the Absolute would prevent other entities having their own unity, and thus would determine their organization. While the absolute provides the principle of limitation necessary for conscious activity, the unity of individual events comes, as we have seen, through the principle of creativity. To this latter 'underlying unity', -- creativity --, the term absolute does not apply.

Because Christian sees the term absolute applying to one aspect of God, and not to some ultimate principle of unity, he is in the position to allow God to participate in the process of events. Christian rightly sees that Whitehead's radically different understanding of the term absolute helps to account for a new theological question. "Unlike that provoked by traditional theology, which forces us to ask: How can an utterly unchanging being have any real knowledge of the changing world?, the question Whitehead's view provokes is: How can a constantly changing being, have a fully determinate experience of the changing world?"6

Christian's answer to this latter question is that
a clear understanding of the absolute pole removes any
possible dilemma. The absolute pole is enjoyed by God
as his 'immediate satisfaction'. But this satisfaction is not complete. The best way to express its
incompleteness is by saying that God's primordial
nature, i.e., the indeterminate unity of pure creativity, objectified in his absolute pole, cannot be
satisfied by any particular unity.7 Of course
Christian does not put it in just these words. He
says, "Now God's aim is at maximum intensity of experience for himself and for the world."8

Whatever particular unity is achieved, God's aim
is toward the still existing infinity of possibilities.
While he holds the past as a particular object and
limitation, he is also the source of an aim which
directs activity beyond a particular satisfaction.9

Only because the absolute pole is the formation
of a particular unity, whose content is not all reality,
can true individuality co-exist with the concept of the
absolute pole. The absolute pole is thus an aspect of
God, and the term absolute cannot be applied as
descriptive of creativity. Christian says, "...God is
neither absolutely complete nor absolutely
independent..."10

In some other Process thinkers, especially in some
of the Process theologians, we will see the suggestion
that the concept of eternal process can be maintained
if a dipolar God is equated with creativity, in a way
that makes the absolute pole the sole principle of
unity. Such a formulation is characterized by the
suggestion that the absolute pole is a principle of a
particular kind of world unification, which is God's
aim. Once this unification is achieved, harmony will
reign, but individuals will continue to interact. This
is tantamount to the concept of a spiritual society
in which there is unity of purpose but individuality
continues. It is a unity 'in which' individuality is

allowed, not a unity 'along with' individuality. Such
an interpretation would imply that finally, if not at
present, God does include the cosmos within himself.
That is, the absolute pole becomes the unity of the
cosmos; the absolute pole becomes a determinate principle of unity.

While this may indeed be a view easier to reconcile with traditional dogmatic positions, Christian
will argue that it is not the Whiteheadian view:

> (a) God is not the cosmos, nor does
> he include (in Hartshorne's sense)
> the cosmos; and (b) his actuality is
> always conditioned though never
> determined by the cosmos. This view
> agrees with traditional theism, against
> traditional pantheism and panentheism,
> in asserting that God is neither
> identical with nor inclusive of the
> world. It agrees with panentheism
> and traditional theism, against
> traditional pantheism, in asserting
> that God transcends the world. And
> it agrees with traditional pantheism
> and panentheism, against traditional
> theism, in asserting that God is
> conditioned by the world.11**

** The reference to Hartshorne concerns a position once
held by him, against Christian's, that God in
Whiteheadian thought could be considered a society of
actual entities...(cf., e.g., MAN'S VISION OF GOD,
pp. 238-240).

Hartshorne, however, modified this view in his
later works. He says, "I once held this doctrine of
absolute simultaneous interaction myself. I cannot
now believe it. But there does seem to be a puzzle.
Contemporaries apparently form a whole which is actual
or concrete, and yet this whole is not a subject...

The points made by Christian in the above quotation each reflect the Process understanding of the term absolute. First, God does not include the cosmos, because there is no ultimate concrete unity of all reality. The absolute pole of God is merely a unity of 'objects' and not of 'events'. Second, God is conditioned but not determined by the cosmos, because events become objects but the absolute pole does not ultimately determine events. The past merely limits present possibilities. On the other hand, if the absolute pole was considered to be an ultimate unity, then God would -- if not at present at least finally -- include the cosmos. Likewise, if the absolute pole was understood to be the determinate organization of activity, events would not condition God.

From our consideration of the works of Christian and Hartshorne we may list a few guidelines for theologians, relative to the Process understanding of God, which should be observed if, in their opinion, a strict application of Whiteheadian meatphysics is to be made:

> (a) The dipolar God should not be equated with creativity, as that would make the term absolute refer to creativity, and suggest that the organization of activity is predetermined.

True, the whole will eventually be in a subject, but not until a long time has passed, unless one conceives deity as somehow escaping relativity principles. (As ubiquitous, God must somehow be a, in principle, unique case.) However, I would deny interaction between God, as in a certain state, and any other individuals in a strictly simultaneous state. On the most concrete level, that of states, there is action, not interaction." (CREATIVE SYNTHESIS AND THE PHILOSOPHIC METHOD. p. 115). Thus Hartshorne and Christian would at present appear to be in agreement.

(b) The absolute pole of God should not be equated with an ultimate principle of unity, as that would suggest that the organization of activity is predetermined.

(c) The principle of unity, of which the absolute pole is an objectification, is indeterminate.

(d) The concept of divine perfection does not depend upon God being an ultimate unity, rather upon God being a concrete unity of the highest possible degree.

(e) God and the world relate through all events, and together participate in creating God's absolute pole.

(f) As the unity of the absolute pole does not include the cosmos, it is not a guarantee of harmony of of the overcoming of evil.

(g) The absolute, as a pole of God, implies the priority of process, but does not lead to an end of that process.

1 Christian, William. AN INTERPRETATION OF WHITEHEAD'S METAPHYSICS. (New York: Yale University Press, 1959). pp. 46-47.
2 ibid. p. 104.   3 p. 117.   4 p. 170.
5 p. 236.   6 p. 296.   7 p. 297.
8 p. 300.   9 p. 335.   10 p. 375.
11 p. 407.

CHAPTER XX

EXAMPLES OF
WHITEHEADIAN PROCESS THEOLOGIANS

In this Chpater we will consider a selection of
the works of Schubert M. Ogden and Daniel Day Williams.
These two writers do not exhaust a category in which
one might include other writers. However, their works
will serve as especially clear illustrations of the
development of some of the theological implications of
Process. We will begin with Ogden, who accepts the
position that God is the objectification of the
creative principle of reality, but that all entities
participate in creativity. He says,

> I hold that the primary use or
> function of 'God' is to refer to
> the objective ground in reality
> itself of our ineradicable con-
> fidence in the final worth of our
> existence. It lies in the nature
> of this confidence to affirm that
> the real whole of which we
> experience ourselves to be parts
> is such as to be worthy of, and
> thus itself to evoke, that very
> confidence. The word 'God' then,
> provides the designation for what-
> ever it is about the experienced
> whole that calls forth and justi-
> fies our original and inescapable
> trust...1

The designation of worth is the fact that God has
existential meaning for man. Such a meaning comes
only from a God understood in terms of the Process dipolar concept. As Hartshorne pointed out, and as
Ogden restates, a totally absolute God means that all
human actions are devoid of worth, i.e., have no
ultimate significance.2

On the other hand, a God who is dipolar gives

meaning, as human events help to create the very unity
which is God's absolute pole. Without God and the
absolute pole, human actions would be random and without significance. The absolute pole is the objectified
specific whole, that does not deny man's contribution.
Just this objectification, according to Ogden, often
appearing in a form called 'myth', is a part of human
experience. He says, "Myth is characterized, first of
all, as a way of representing linguistically a basic
field of human experience -- namely, that field in
which each of us is aware of himself and the world as
parts of an encompassing whole."3 Indeed we can only
account for our feeling of the whole because of the
absolute pole, which is an object of that feeling.
Ogden is in close agreement with Whitehead that
physical feelings in man always precede conceptual
feelings.

    Ogden's point is that once myth about God is
viewed in terms of the Process understanding of God's
dipolar nature, the myth is 'De-mythologized', i.e.,
it is related to human experience. The Process understanding of the term absolute allows us to get behind
myth to the existential situation which it objectifies;
namely, that events have worth because they influence
the trend of formation in the whole of reality.4

    Having argued that the Process understanding of
the absolute relates God to the existential situation,
Ogden fully realizes that the price of this formulation
is a necessary re-interpretation of Christology. Ogden
was a student of Bultmann, but he felt that his teacher
was not prepared to fully de-mythologize Christ.5
Ogden's Christology relates to our interests, because
it is his understanding of the term absolute, which
makes it impossible to assign overall significance to
a single event. The absolute pole, the unity of the
past, is made up of all events. It is this whole
which allows man to see his worth, All human actions
are 'redeemed',i.e., given worth as part of the whole,
in God. "The claim 'only in Jesus Christ' must be
interpreted to mean, not that God acts to redeem only
in the history of Jesus and in no other history, but

that the only God who redeems any history -- although
he in fact redeems every history -- is the God whose
redemptive action is decisively re-presented in the
word that Jesus speaks and is."6

Jesus clearly does not present a new order of
reality. He does not represent a culmination of one
plan for all history. Rather, according to Ogden, he
shows us that all history is redeemed.7

From man's point of view we are related to creativity only as it is objectified in God. As redeemer of
history, God is the actual concrete reality which gives
human actions worth; and God is creator in the sense
that without his concrete reality creativity would not
be available. "The purpose of Jesus' ministry, whether
of word or deed, was far less to speak about man and
his relationship to God -- although he did that, too --
than to speak of that relationship so that it itself
could be encountered in its full existential reality."8
In other words, Jesus shows that we are all of God.
God's absolute pole is made up of our redeemed history.
We participate in a whole through our contributions to
that whole.

Ogden argues that his understanding is sufficient
to make Jesus a decisive act.9 On the other side, Jesus
reveals that all history is redemptive history; his is
not a uniquely redemptive history. Clearly this is a
departure from many other Christologies, which do
think of Jesus' as a uniquely redemptive history.
Ogden's alternative position concerning Jesus results
in large part from the fact that the term absolute in
Process must be understood as referring to a unity of
the whole of the past, and not to a particular predetermined unity, which can be accomplished through a
single event.

Ogden's formulations also influence eschatology.10
The promise of the reality of God becomes the redem-
ption of all history. It is not the promise of a
particular end to history. As we said, all technical
references to 'last things' lose their meaning if the

absolute pole is not a particular ultimate unity -- either predetermined or yet to be finally determined.

Having briefly considered how Process thought influenced the theology of Ogden, we will consider some of the ideas introduced by Daniel Day Williams. His book THE SPIRIT AND THE FORMS OF LOVE is an attempt to give meaning to the concept of divine love through the application of Process thinking. Here we will also see the particular influence of the Process understanding of the term absolute. Williams says,

> When we search for the unity of
> love admist those forms we discover
> that love has a history. The spirit
> is not a static ideal but a creative
> power which participates in the life
> it informs. Here is the key to
> everything we shall be saying in the
> discussion of love.11

What Williams calls 'the spirit of love' appears to have the very qualities heretofore associated with the Whiteheadian principle of creativity. Indeed, we will see that he makes love meaningful by substituting it for that principle. He begins his very interesting book with a discussion of the history of the understanding of love as it developed within the western Christian tradition. He speaks of three historical formulations which he calls the Augustinian, the Franciscan, and the Evangelical or Reformation concepts.12 His descriptions of these positions, for our purposes, are not as important as the fact that he finds it necessary to reject each of them.

However, he is most sympathetic to Augustine's formulation. Nevertheless, Williams sees that the Augustinian concept of God is inconsistent with his understanding of love. Williams says, "What Augustine does is to conceive God the Creator and Redeemer with all the absolute aspects which neo-Platonism has ascribed to the transcendental and changeless One."13 Williams cannot accept the neo-Platonic concept for the following reasons: (1) It denies human freedom; (2) It makes the new impossible; (3) It makes the human world of change inferior; and, (4) It makes it impossible to account for the Incarnation and Atonement.14 Indeed, says Williams, love can have no meaning apart from individuality, freedom, action, and suffering, causality, and impartiality -- the very things which a neo-Platonic understanding of God as the Absolute makes impossible for God.15

If we wish to see God participating in love, we must have a formulation in which his creative and redemptive roles do not depend upon his being 'absolute' in what Williams calls the neo-Platonic sense. Williams wants to make a distinction between God as in some sense absolute, and God as participating in the spirit of love. The way in which he formulates his position on love is to make the term absolute refer, not to an ultimate plan or unity, but rather to a fexible state. "The Kingdom of God is the goal of his creation; but we need not conceive the Kingdom as a fixed 'state of being' toward which things tend."16

Of course Williams has introduced theological terms to express his point, but behind these we can see the influence of the Process understanding of the absolute pole. Both the Kingdom of God and the absolute pole are unities of relationships between God and man. Both the Kingdom and the absolute pole are said to fulfill God. Neither are fixed states, although both are objective realities. Thus Williams makes a distinction between the unity of love in which all entities participate, and the unity of God's Kingdom.17

For Williams man participates in the spirit of love, just as for Whitehead all entities participate in the principle of creativity. The term absolute does not apply to love. Love is not a concrete unity or a principle of limitation, rather it is a dynamic principle of communion, i.e., freedom and responsiveness. On the other hand, the term absolute would apply to a factor of God's being that is in relation to every creature. No other entity relates to 'all' entities.

The term absolute is applied to God in terms of his unifying of relationships. Because of God's unique relatedness, no other entity, Williams points out, has the exact same experience as does God. The human individual's participation in love is here described as God's will that man should commune with him. This is God's will because he himself participates in the principle of love. "Man, created in god's image, is created for participation in the infinite life of communion within the everlasting creativity of God."18

Such an analysis says Williams is proven true by the fact that it fulfills a basic human longing. "Begin with the assertion that the fundamental human craving is to belong, to count in the community of being, to have one's freedom in and with the response of others, to enjoy God as one who makes us members of one society."19 For Williams the absolute pole or Kingdom of God is not only a unity, but it is also a principle of limitation. He says, "Something must re-create the capacity to belong in the society of God's creatures so that man finds his security in giving himself to the service and enjoyment of God and His Kingdom as the ultimate context of every human love."20

Love is itself an unlimited potential for new possibilities of relatedness. However, man requires some limitation on his possibilities. That is, man must have an ultimate context to which he can refer every human love. This context is God's Kingdom. Thus God's Kingdom serves both as a unity and as a principle of limitation. It can rightly be called 'absolute' by the Process understanding.

Based on Williams understanding of love and the Kingdom of God, the Incarnation and Atonement have new meaning.21 Jesus, according to Williams, does not make man's relationship to God possible, rather he demonstrates the nature of God's relationship to mankind. God relates to man not in a single act, but through all events. Therefore, of atonement Williams says, "Atonement is creation."22 He also says, "Love is not possession, but participation."23

The Kingdom of God, which Jesus spoke about, is not a future state in which men are finally brought into relationship with God. Instead, it already exists for all who are aware of their participation with God in creative acts of love. Furthermore, participation with God is constantly renewed as more possibilities of love are realized by man. 'Atonement is creation' means that as human events enter into the unity of God's absolute pole, that unity becomes ever new -- a new community of love.

If the Kingdom was thought of as a concrete future state, it would be a predetermined unity within God. However, as Williams said, 'Love is not possession but participation.' Man could not participate in something already determined, because his action would have no ultimate significance. If man's actions have no ultimate significance, then he does not relate to God.

On the other hand, it is because of the significance which the absolute pole, i.e., the Kingdom, allows man's actions to have that atonement becomes possible. Apart from God there could be no significant acts by William's formulation.

In summary it may be helpful to review how Ogden and Williams attempt to formulate in theological terms the philosophical guidelines which we indicated were necessary in order to adopt the Whiteheadian understanding of God. The key problem, of course, is to avoid equating God with creativity in such a way that the term absolute must logically refer to a determinate plan of unity. Ogden avoids this by suggesting, much like Christian, that God's wholeness is the objectification of man's participation in the creation of the unity of the universe. Williams, somewhat differently, speaks of love as the essential creative reality in which both God and man participate. The purpose in either case is to avoid making God an impassible absolute; and the way they do this is to understand God's absoluteness as somehow distinct from a general principle of unity in which all entities, including God, participate.

201

For both men God's unity is understood as a
redeemed history; that is, human history given worth
because it participates in the shaping of reality. All
history becomes the history of the relationship between
God and the world, because of God's redemptive act in
making it a unity. The making of this unity is a
creative function shared by God and man. God's
further creative function is to open for men new
possibilities for relations beyond any particular unity.

The absolute pole, the particular unity of redeemed history, is called by Ogden the object of the
experience of the whole, and by Williams the Kingdom
of God. Because of the nature of the absolute pole,
neither of these are static. As all history is
redeemed, Jesus can hardly be called its Redeemer.
Ogden argues, therefore, that his role is to re-present
for our conscious awareness that which is implicitly
revealed to all men in their feelings of worth for
human actions. Likewise, Williams says that Jesus
exemplifies that a relationship of love is the essential nature of God. In neither case does Jesus'
incarnation totally change the nature of the God-world
relationship; it merely enriches it -- perhaps to the
highest possible degree.

The above does not suggest that these men want to
play-down Jesus' importance. Once man sees his worth
clearly objectified, or sees the principle of love
humanly objectified, his actions are changed. He will
respond to Jesus by acting in a way increasingly com-
patible with human worth or love.

Finally, not only is all history redeemed, but it
is redeemed now. Eschatology takes on a present rather
than a future meaning. Yet this emphasis on the
present opens, rather than closes, the future. History
by its very nature continues infinitely. Man, according to Williams, is created for communion, i.e,
relationships with God, and this fact demands a continuing history. God did not create toward any end less
than infinite enrichment.

What we observe in the above summary is exactly the Process influence on theology which we suggested in our consideration of Hartshorne and Christian. The Process understanding of the term absolute significantly changes eschatology, Christology and soteriology. In fact these changes seem too radical to be reconciled with traditional dogmatic positions.

The theologians we have considered were prepared to make the adjustment in theological thinking necessary to adopt a Process position. We shall now turn to other theologians, who are greatly attracted by certain Process formulations, but who find it necessary to compromise the Process position when it comes to accepting the distinction between a principle of unity in which all entities participate, and a concrete unity in God's absolute pole.

1 Ogden, Schubert M. THE REALITY OF GOD. (New York: Harper, 1966). p. 37.
2 ibid. p. 51.   3 p. 114.
4 Ogden, Schubert M. CHRIST WITHOUT MYTH. (London: Collins, 1962). p. 30.
5 ibid. p. 167.
6 Ogden. REALITY OF GOD. p. 173.   7 ibid. pp. 185-186
8 Ogden. CHRIST WITHOUT MYTH. p. 190.
9 Ogden. REALITY OF GOD. p. 186.
10 ibid. p. 210.
11 Williams, Daniel Day. THE SPIRIT AND THE FORMS OF LOVE. (London: James Nisbet,1968). p. 4
12 ibid. pp. 53-76.   13 p. 92.   14 pp. 95-100.
15 pp. 114-122.   16 p. 135.   17 p. 137
18 p. 138.   19 p. 146.   20 p. 149.
21 p. 185.   22 p. 187.   23 p. 209.

CHAPTER XXI

LIONEL THORNTON'S
INCARNATIONAL THEOLOGY

Hartshorne, Christian, Ogden and Williams demonstrate writers who reject any interpretation of Whiteheadian thought which makes the term absolute refer to a universal principle of activity, rather than to an aspect of God. Accepting this distinction causes its supporters to introduce several significant changes into theological formulations. Althought we have indicated our preference for the foregoing interpretation of the absolute's reference, in spite of its implications for theology, we have also said that an alternative interpretation of the term absolute is held by other theologians, who also state that their theologies reflect Process.

Equating a dipolar God with creativity is necessarily a contradiction. Once the absolute pole is associated with an ultimate principle of unity, God can no longer relate to the world. Unfortunately, our formulation of the reason for this distinction between God and creativity cannot easily be discovered in Whitehead's writings. We know from Cobb's excellent study that Whitehead appears to change his mind as to the specific relationship between God and creativity. And, Whitehead does not specifically explain the stages in his thinking which led to his conclusions.

Nevertheless, we can show that because of the necessity of understanding the term absolute as referring to a pole of specific unity in God, the alternative of simply equating God and creativity produces a very subtle form of determinism. In other words, the influence of the concept absolute is finally that which makes it essential to determine one's position in respect to a distinction between the dipolar God and creativity. We will begin our illustration of those who do not make this distinction with the writings of Lionel Thornton.

Thornton is our choice for several good reasons.
First, his work THE INCARNATE LORD, with which we will
be concerned, is an attempt to develop a theology
specifically consistent with Whitehead's works up to
PROCESS AND REALITY. Second, he closely follows
Whiteheadian thought at nearly every point except that
he does equate God with creativity. Third, in spite
of generally great likenesses between Thornton's development of his position and the development made by
Hartshorne, Christian, Ogden and Williams, some of the
key theological points do in the end differ from the
latter four's positions, because of his interpretation
of creativity. Fourth, the results of his equating
the dipolar God with creativity are deterministic
conclusions.

If we can show that it is the understanding of the
absolute and creativity that is the chief explanation
for the above, we will have made an important inroad
in distinguishing two major branches of Process theology that developed out of Whitehead's writings.
Furthermore, we hope to give evidence for the suggestion that the reason for equating God with creativity
is that it appears to some theologians to allow
reconciliation between Process and some other theological trends.

In the foregoing Chapters we have made quite clear
that what we mean by Process and determinism make them
incompatible. To say that one combines Process and
deterministic qualities is to suggest some gross inconsistencies. We merely want to show how an association
of the term absolute with creativity produces these
inconsistencies, and why, from a theological point of
view, certain writer may easily get caught in inconsistency with regard to the use of these concepts.

Process theology has a very difficult time in
dealing with Christology. However, Thornton feels that
the formulations developed by emergence and Process
clarify, rather than confuse, the meaning of the
incarnation. In his book THE INCARNATE LORD Thornton
suggests that there were three possible theological-

philosophical systems which might have served the needs
of his day: Hegelian Idealism, Evolutionary Mechanism,
and Emergence-Process. The first two possibilities,
he suggests, cannot finally account for the Christian
experience of the incarnation.1 He understands that
the doctrine of the incarnation wants a culminating
historical event, which does not prevent process, but
which nonetheless gives meaning to the process. The
analogy of organism, he says, used by emergence and
Process, gives a model which makes sense out of these
two demands.2 Referring in particular to the concept
of emergent levels, he says,

> At every step the whole which is
> typical for that grade is some-
> thing more than a collection of
> its parts. The parts are held
> together in a unity; and the part-
> icular principle of unity which is
> there manifested is the highest
> law of being in that level. It is
> the distinctive principle which
> informs entities on that level.3

The above relates to the concept of organism because
when we consider "...unity in complexity, of wholeness
pervading a variety of parts, which we conceive the
organism as possessing at any given moment of time,
then we have a concept of the complete life-story of
the organism as a concrete entity immanent in the
spatiotemporal succession of events, yet transcending
it."4

The principle of organism Thornton refers to as
the 'Eternal Order'.5 Man adds Thornton is the highest
level of emergence because of his participation
directly in the eternal order through his consciousness
of it.6 The transcendent reality of the unity of the
eternal order fills the incarnational demand for the
present fact of ultimate unity. The continued individuality within the eternal order allows for an on-going
process.

The eternal order is understood as a field of change composed alike of unity and diversity. The field of change is set in what Thornton calls 'Absolute Actuality'. And he equates God with absolute actuality.7 God is the all-embracing, changeless being who includes activity within himself. Activity itself is composed of an aspect of all-embracing unity and of individuality. Therefore, says Thornton, we can think of God or Absolute Being, because he is revealed through the eternal order.

The above is Thornton's analysis of process. Before going on to see how he applies it to theology, we may consider its relation to the Whiteheadian position. Clearly the eternal order is dipolar, rather like Whitehead's God is dipolar. However, the eternal order is not God. God is the changeless absolute actuality which includes the eternal order. God himself could not be dipolar. Thornton is aware of this when he says, "For religion the ultimate reality is not primarily unity or absoluteness or an eternal order, but God in His concrete individuality."8

Thornton admits that we experience God as if he was what we have described as the eternal order, i.e., as being dipolar. Here Thornton and Whitehead would be nearly at one. If Thornton said that God was the eternal order, which pointed to an indeterminate principle of activity, they might be in full agreement. Indeed, Thornton builds further groundwork for just such agreement by the suggestion that the eternal order has to serve as an object for man, or man could not know it.9

It seems that we are almost on the verge of being told, in Whiteheadian fashion, that God is the eternal order, which is really the objectification of a principle -- perhaps the principle of creativity. However, at this point it becomes clear that Thornton and Whitehead are not talking along the same lines. The language sounds similar, but Thornton does not draw a distinction between the unity in God, and a principle of unity in which all entities participate.

208

According to Thornton, the objectified eternal
order reveals to man that there is a unity in which he
does not participate.10 In other words, Thornton says
that the concept of absolute actuality, which is the
changeless principle behind the activity of the eternal
order, also has a concrete content. The only way to
provide for this is to say that the eternal order, the
agent of the revelation, and the absolute actuality,
the content of the revelation, are both God.

This is different from Whitehead, who if he used
Thornton's terms, would have to say that God is the
eternal order and must be a concrete object of physical
feeling; and that this feeling gives rise of a conceptual feeling of an indeterminate principle of creativity
in which both God and the world participate. Because,
according to Process, activity can only be explained if
there is true diversity; and true diversity demands
that all entities have their own identity.

Thornton's formulations, on the other hand, do
suggest a god beyond God -- an absolutely ultimate God
behind the unity in activity. The absolute God of
ultimate reality must necessarily be a particular,
concrete and predetermined unity. Thornton admits this
by saying,

> For the eternal order provides the
> principles of unity which determine
> the directive movement of the organic
> universe, of man and of history. But
> these principles of unity, while
> adequate in their totality to determine
> the directive movement of the cosmic
> process, are not adequate to provide
> a goal in which that process can come
> to rest. The process passes beyond
> each of them; and the self-determining
> activity of man, which is the highest
> of these principles in the series, is
> by its very nature self-transcending
> and therefore incapable of providing
> a last term for the process.11

A true Whiteheadian would say, the eternal order does not provide for an end to the process, because the process itself is the ultimate. If process is not the ultimate, then there can be no real process at all. The very suggestion of a goal to the process means that the concept absolute has been understood as referring to an ultimate and predetermining principle of unity. As Ogden pointed out, a formulation such as Thornton's suggests that process occurs within the absolute; but this statement is inconsistent. By definition, something which is absolute is what it is. If it is said to be a unity of ultimate reality, then there is no room for the individuality necessary for change and activity.

We now see that Thornton has made the absolute pole a unification of all reality by equating the dipolar God with an ultimate principle of process. The implication of this he rightly interprets to be that process has an end. However, he misses the point that if this is true, then no real process could occur at all. Furthermore, we are now ready to understand why Thornton fell into this inconsistency. If the eternal order reveals God and is God, it means that Thornton can suggest quite easily that the name given to the 'person' of God as agent of revelation is Jesus Christ.12

For Thornton Jesus Christ (embodied eternal order) functions much like God in the Whiteheadian system.13 That is, the pole of unity in Jesus, like that in Whitehead's God, is a unity of history which serves as a goal for man by being the unity in which man can participate toward shaping reality. Jesus is, for Thornton, the passive aspect of an otherwise impassible God. While this passive aspect is quite clearly described in Process terms as having an absolute and a relative pole, the fact that it is embodied in a higher absolute actuality renders it contradictory. If God does not reveal himself as himself, then he does not relate in himself. In true Process a mediator between God and the world is not a consistent idea, as long as such a formulation implies that behind relationships is a principle that does not participate in relationships.

In a last attempt to try and assure the reader that he does not want to suggest divine impassibility, Thornton looks to the Trinity to argue that God as absolute actuality does have relationships within himself. God he argues is a complex unity of at least three natures.14

This is really not a solution at all. Williams pointed out that relations demand more than internal individuality if they are to be authentic. They also require freedom, action, and suffering, causality and impartiality. And it is exactly these things that the term absolute, used to refer to one aspect of ultimate reality, does not allow. Whatever sort of relations occur within the God of Thornton's theological system, they are relations that have no analogy to human experience.

We have seen that to a point Process formulations serve other, more traditional concepts of theology quite well. At the point of the distinction between the absolute pole and an indeterminate principle of unity, the would-be Process theologian faces real difficulties. This fact, as we have seen illustrated, is especially true in areas such as Christology and eschatology. Only by changing from the Process understanding was Thornton able to speak of a goal for all process, and of a unique place for Jesus within his system. Yet this change is far from insignificant, as it re-opens many of the very dilemmas --especially determinism -- which Process was eager to avoid.

Thornton is interesting because his work is the first attempt at true Process theology. Also it illustrates many of the problems that may arise for a Process theology. Finally it represents the beginning of the second theological trend that came out of the Whiteheadian philosophy.

1 Thornton, Lionel Spencer. THE INCARNATE LORD.
   (London: Longmanns Green, 1928). p. 22.
2 ibid. p. 32.   3 p. 37.   4 p. 41.
5 pp. 56-57.   6 p. 57.   7 p. 86.
8 p. 94.   9 p. 127.   10 p. 151.
11 pp. 313-315   12 p. 223.   13 p. 214.

CHAPTER XXII

NORMAN PITTENGER'S THEOLOGY

In his book CHRISTOLOGY RECONSIDERED Pittenger
says of Thornton,

> While he is prepared in the earlier
> portions of THE INCARNATE LORD to
> accept and to use (to great effect)
> the philosophy of process developed
> by Professor Alfred North Whitehead,
> he draws back as soon as he comes to
> the consideration of the sense in
> which Jesus may be styled final and
> the way in which it may be said of
> Jesus that he transcends other
> revelatory activity of God. At
> this point, but not before or else-
> where, he feels obligated to insist
> that the whole Logos, as we might
> describe it, is intruded into the
> world in the incarnation of the
> Word in Jesus Christ; thus he
> succeeds, quite contrary to what
> must have been his intention at the
> beginning, in making that event
> partake of an entirely different
> order from all the rest of the
> divine revelatory activity in the
> creation.1

It is very important for Process not to think of
Jesus as the sole or entirely special revelation of
God, since, as we have illustrated, the concept of a
dipolar God demonstrates that God relates through all
events. Therefore, Pittenger takes the alternative
of suggesting that the relation between God and the
man Jesus, and God and other events, is not a difference in kind but in 'degree'.2

He becomes even more specific about Jesus'
relationship to God by saying that Jesus more fully

than any other event fulfils God's aim; namely, that
the world should realize its deepest potentialities.3
In order to develop a model for what it means to say
that Jesus realized God's aim to a unique degree,
Pittenger says: "Rather, the model which we shall find
most satisfactory for understanding Jesus of Nazareth
is that of a man who with his own distinctive qualities
and gifts is yet most deeply conscious of the history
out of which he emerged, is profoundly aware of his
relationships with his fellow men and his responsibility towards them, and is most seminal (we might put
it) in providing opportunities for further and richer
development for others in the years which follow his
necessarily limited period of life in this world."4

In the above Pittenger has succeeded in describing
Jesus as exactly like the Whiteheadian God. First,
Jesus is said to hold deeply in consciousness the
history out of which he emerged; but as Pittenger
earlier suggested that Jesus emerged out of all history,
Jesus must hold all history in deep consciousness. All
of the past is the content of the absolute pole of God.
Second, Jesus is profoundly aware of relationships.
Indeed, the uniqueness of God's relative pole is that
it is relative to the highest possible degree. Finally
Jesus provides opportunities for the future. According
to Pittenger the scope of this provision has a divine
dimension. In fact he calls Jesus 'God incognito.'

> For Christian faith, at any rate,
> if man is to see God 'plain' it must
> be under the incognito of manhood,
> which is why Christians believe that
> God is incarnate, enmanned, in the
> human life of the man Jesus. We do
> not see God 'plain' in nature, but
> we see something of what he does and
> how he does it, under that natural
> incognito. And from what he does
> and how he does it, we learn some-
> thing of what he is.5

Pittenger has clearly made some changes from

214

Thornton's position. What the changes amount to, however, is that instead of doing what Thornton does, and make Jesus break-in on history, Pittenger says that Jesus himself emerges out of history. He is a newly emergent level.6 Of course Thornton talks about emergence, but, as we saw, his Christological formulations indicate that he does not take seriously the implications of Jesus himself emerging. That is, he breaks the continuity of history with Jesus. We might say that Jesus, for Pittenger, is Thornton's eternal order with a real history. That is, Jesus is God fully revealing himself through a process of history. Process is thus the content of revelation, and its agent.7

If we are right that Jesus is presented as God, then in Jesus, God is revealing himself. We therefore get back to Thornton's point that, through Jesus, God is revealed as the ultimate process itself. To be more specific, Jesus reveals a dipolar God, who is equated with the ultimate process of the universe. Indeed we are told by Pittenger that God has two aspects:

> Whatever 'absolutes' we attribute
> to God consist in his unfailing
> capacity to be himself, even while
> he is also intimately related to
> all that goes on and may go on.
> He is indefatigable Love, luring
> and attracting others to new and
> untried modes for love's expression.8

We have too often repeated that the absolute pole is for Process a specific concrete unity as Pittenger implies in the above. However, if God as dipolar is the content of revelation, this means that his absolute pole is a specific ultimate unity. Indeed at one point Pittenger interprets God as being the source of creativity:

> He is also the 'chief exemplification'

215

(in Whitehead's phrase) of all principles necessary to describe the
world. Hence as the chief exempli-
fication and the ultimate source of
creativity, he is the creator (not
the artificaer, but the artist or
poet) and the redeemer (the one who
saves all that can be saved) of the
world, as we have presupposed and on
more than one occasion explicitly
indicated. God is the center of the
cosmos, not man.9

Interestingly, Pittenger realizes that if God is the
source of creativity, then universal process must have
a final goal. He says, "The final goal is 'in' God --
in fellowship with cosmic Love to know the enabling
and ennobling of all that we have in us to become."10

By changing Thornton's concept of the eternal
order to a concept of Jesus himself as an emergent
level of reality, Pittenger has certainly moved a bit
further from a dogmatic position. Yet, it is clear
that he does not fit into a Whiteheadian position as
regards the use of the term absolute. As we have seen,
for Pittenger Jesus is God's revelation of himself as
the principle of creativity. In which case the
absolute pole becomes a pole of ultimate reality. A
distinction between the two forms of unity is not
maintained.

The advantage that Pittenger's formulation has for
his theology is that it appears to allow him to retain
the idea of a God that relates, without disallowing a
goal for the process. In talking about churches he
says, "Nothing that is good need be altered in content,
but a wholly new spirit will enter into the life of a
congregation that is thoroughly conscious of the
stupendous fact that it is a 'cell' of the Body of
Christ, with the vocation to be Christ to the particular community in which it is set."11 As we saw
before, the analogy of the Body of Christ can be interpreted to mean that, as head of the body, Christ

becomes a singularly dominate event so that the individuality of any other events, or societies of events, within the body, are subordinated to the good of the whole. The fact that subordination, as Pittenger suggests, might occur with the consent of the occasions involved does not mean that such a structure could in fact exist. Indeed Hartshorne and Christian suggest that the harmony implied in such a formulation is not possible from the Whiteheadian viewpoint.

We must conclude that, while Pittenger is not a traditional dogmatic theologian, his Christology, in particular, is not immediately persuasive as being a contribution to consistent Whiteheadian Process thought. Unless the issues sorrounding the difference between creativity and the absolute pole can be more satisfactorily related to Christology, it remains a dilemma for Process theologians.

1 Pittenger, Norman. CHRISTOLOGY RECONSIDERED. (London: SCM Press, 1970). p. 19.
2 ibid. p. 86.   3 p. 83.   4 p. 70.
5 Pittenger, Norman. GOD'S WAY WITH MAN. (London: Hodder & Soughton, 1969). p. 46.
6 ibid. p. 144.
7 Pittenger. CHRISTOLOGY RECONSIDERED. p. 142.
8 Pittenger, Norman. THE CHRISTIAN CHURCH AS SOCIAL PROCESS. (London: Epworth Press, 1971). p. 121.
9 Pittenger. GOD'S WAY WITH MAN. p. 171.
10 Pittenger. THE CHRISTIAN CHURCH AS SOCIAL PROCESS. p. 60.
11 Pittenger, Norman. THE HISTORIC FAITH AND A CHANGING WORLD. (New York: Oxford,1950). p. 137.

CHAPTER XXIII

BERNARD MELAND AND
JOHN COBB

We will conclude our discussions of Whiteheadian
influenced Process theologies with Bernard Meland's
THE REALITIES OF FAITH, and John Cobb's A CHRISTIAN
NATURAL THEOLOGY. In terms of the implications of the
concepts of creativity and absoluteness, we will find
these men closer to a strict Whiteheadian positon, as
we have developed it, than either Thornton or
Pittenger.

Like several of Pittenger's works, Meland's THE
REALITIES OF FAITH places a strong emphasis upon
establishing a unique role for Jesus while maintaining
a dipolar concept of God. Pittenger, we recall,
attempted to modify Thornton's Christology by arguing
for the emergence of Jesus out of history, rather than
accepting a sudden entry of the 'logos' into history.
The latter tends to make the incarnation the sole
event relating God and man. Meland goes even further
than Pittenger in modifying Christology by suggesting
that before Jesus the Hebraic concept of covenant
also revealed a God who relates to man -- a dipolar
God: "...the covenant relationship -- the notion that
God comes to man in a personal encounter and establishes a relationship with his people, binding them
together in a mutual pact of obligation and responsiveness. It is a relationship correlating faithfulness
and freedom."1 This idea of a relationship which
represents mutual freedom, Meland takes as central to
the Process conception of God. He says that it is an
attempt to respond to the issue of the Many and the
One.

However, for Meland, the events of the Cross and
Resurrection give Western Christianity a special and
distinctive understanding of the principle of relatedness implied by the covenant. "Together these two
themes provide the clue to what is distinctive in our
Western Christian conception of goodness, which implies

an attitude of abandon toward the cost of relationships
and its corollary, an investment of self, with confidence in the ultimate resolution of the crises that may
follow from such a course, issuing in possible death
and momentary defeat."2

According to Meland, Jesus illustrates that the
cost of relationship -- the giving of self -- is re-
warded by a resulting unity which affords the
individual a depth he could not otherwise have. Jesus'
self-sacrifice opened up new possibilities of relationship between man and God, just as the formation of any
unity opens up new possibilities for relationship.3
Of course, one might well remain consistent to
Whiteheadian thought, and nevertheless maintain that
Jesus' actions opened more possibilities for relationships than the actions of any other single entity.

To this point nothing that Meland has suggested
would deny that God himself relates to man through all
events. In fact Meland clearly said that God did
relate to man through all of history. Nevertheless,
as he gives more attention to Christology, the nature
of God's relatedness becomes less consistent with the
Whiteheadian understanding of dipolarity. In order to
analyze this fact we must begin by looking more carefully at Meland's use of the concept of relatedness.

To relate consciously, says Meland, is to gain a
vision of the possibilities that come through relationships. It is a vision of unity, which might even be
called a faith:

> There is no faith that may claim
> ultimacy in the sense of possessing
> or conveying absolute truth. Yet
> there is no faith devoid of ulti-
> mate reality in what it bodies forth.
> This is to say that all faiths are
> relative in what they are able to
> embody and express of ultimate
> reality. The point that we need to
> grasp if we are to assume a

constructive stance in this new
imagery of thought is that relativity is itself a witness to
ultimacy.4

The above is consistent with the Whiteheadian concept of the absolute pole of God. The absolute pole
could be called an object of faith having a concrete
content, but its content would not be all of reality.
Therefore, one cannot speak of ultimate, absolute
truth, i.e., a particular ultimate unity. However,
the above quotation must also be understood by considering what he means by the term 'relativity'. Of
particular usefulness is the following;

But relativity does not necessarily
mean the loss of all decisive norms
or of decision in the judgment of
meaning or value... On the contrary,
it denies simply the reality of
arbitrary absolutes, and invests
absoluteness in reality itself,
wherever it occurs, under whatever
guise it appears.5

In Meland's description of relativity, there is
the equating of the dipolar God with 'ultimate
reality'. It is true, according to Whitehead, that
some factor unifies present reality. Relativity is a
real cosmic factor precisely because God's absolute
pole does not include the present subjective aim of
all entities. The principle of individuality is
rigorously maintained by the denial of simultaneity
between contemporary occasions. The absolute pole of
God must be a unity of all non-contemporary occasions,
and not of all reality. Otherwise, if the absolute
pole is a unity of contemporary occasions, there is no
real individuality. To say that Process 'invests
absoluteness in reality itself, wherever it occurs,
under whatever guise it appears,' and to equate God
with ultimate reality, means that one must be very
careful how the term 'reality' is used. If reality *
means 'objective' reality, well and good. However,

if reality is used in the broader sense to include the cosmos, the formulation is inconsistent. As we have often suggested, to ascribe absoluteness to ultimate reality -- Whitehead's creativity -- by equating it with a dipolar God is by implication to contradict the very possibility of activity.

Unfortunately, in the quotation immediately preceding the above, Meland uses the term ultimate reality, and says that relativity is a witness to ultimacy. If he means that relativity, with a part-icular, i.e., not arbitrary, unity, is witness to the ultimate reality of a dipolar God, who also has a particular, not an arbitrary unity, then he in fact falls into the trap of making the term absolute refer to an ultimate unity.

It again is Christology that sets the trap. As Jesus is equated with relativity by Meland, and as God is equated with the ultimate, we have another case of God being equated with creativity. Such an equation always means that the absolute pole of God functions in a predetermining way. In other words, the unity with God which Jesus reveals is an ultimate unity functioning as a divine plan.

We already have evidence that Meland equates God with the ultimate. Further evidence is his use of Imago Dei in company with the concept of God as the Creator.6

In his formulation there is no clear evidence that he takes seriously the Whiteheadian point that man is not only a creature, but is also a co-creator with God. The reason for this is that by making God the ultimate reality, Meland has equated the dipolar God with creativity itself; making God the sole creator.

If man does not directly participate in creativity then Jesus, as the principle of relativity, according to Meland, reveals and makes possible participation. He speaks of Jesus as revealing a 'new creation' which emerged from history.7

Because Jesus is equated with relativity, it becomes similar to Thornton's eternal order; and ultimate reality to Thornton's absolute actuality. That is, Meland seems to be saying that the ultimate principle is a God who relates, but who also has a relative pole. However, as we have seen, just this formulation disregards the implications of the term absolute applying to God's pole of unity. The absolute pole is a particular unity and a principle of limitation. If the ultimate has a particular unity, then that unity predetermines the plan and goal of all reality. Jesus thus becomes the revelation of a particular plan and goal, and the new creation is thought of as a final unity in which relations continue. Such an idea is contradictory.

We will now turn to John Cobb, who in his work A CHRISTIAN NATURAL THEOLOGY, argues in the Whiteheadian tradition, that God has a dipolar nature.[8] On the one hand, says Cobb, God does have an aspect of 'otherness', but at the same time he is present in events. Indeed, according to Cobb, God is unlike any other entity in that he participates in all events. Cobb arrives at his understanding of dipolarity by starting with the assumption that while Whitehead thinks of God as a conscious actual entity, one is better to think of God as a living person.[9] What makes a living person special for Cobb is a 'soul' This soul is not described as an underlying substance. Rather it is the sequence of experiences that constitute the unity of history.[10]

The concrete content of the divine soul would be the unity of God's experiences -- which in fact means every event.   In keeping with this understanding of soul, God, says Cobb, must be a society of actual occasions, i.e. he must share the immediacy of all actual occasions.[11] We might here remember the distinction that Christian made between God as a unity of past events, i.e. objects, and present events, i.e., events of immediacy, which are not included in God's absolute pole. Unlike Christian, Cobb is suggesting that God is a unity of objects and events. Even Cobb himself admits that some other Process thinkers would reject this position.12

We have established that the pole of unity in God is what Cobb would call a soul. However, as God also has a relative pole, there must be a diversity of events or potential events which gives the divine nature its complex character. Cobb accepts this point, and suggests that God should be called dipolar because he is the ultimate source of both unity and diversity,

> Whitehead explicitly explains that creativity is in his system what the prime matter is in Aristotle, namely, the material cause. This suggests, correctly, that the problem of a doctrine of creation in Whitehead is much like that in a philosophy based on Aristotle; the role of the creator is to provide form for a reality given to him.13

Cobb's analysis of Whitehead's position is not totally justifiable. Activity, as ultimate, implies for Whitehead that individuality must always be maintained along with unity. That is, there must be a distinction between the unity of God's absolute pole and a principle of unity in which all entities participate. Therefore, only the past is included in the absolute pole, while the present retains its multiple character. God, it is also true, must work within creativity as a given. However, what Cobb neglects to mention is that creativity for Whitehead is not shaped by God alone; rather the form which creativity takes is also contributed to by man. It was to assure man's participation in creativity that led Whitehead to draw the distinction between creativity and God.

Cobb would not fully agree with this distinction:

> We have already seen that the decisive element in the initiation of each

actual occasion is the granting to
that occasion of an initial aim.
Since Whitehead attributes this
function to God, it seems that,
to a greater degree than Whitehead
intended, God must be conceived as
being the reason that entities occur
at all as well as determining the
limit within which they may
achieve their own form.14

What Cobb suggests is that God himself provides
the necessary multiplicity for activity to take place.
In other words, God is equated with creativity. In all
of this Cobb has somewhat ignored the implications of
the absolute pole. When a dipolar God is equated with
creativity, the absolute pole becomes a specific unity
of all reality. Once an ultimate unity has been
accepted, the only process that one could talk about is
a process within the absolute pole. Such a formulation
suggests that process can take place without true
individuality. That is, to use Cobb's terms, God's
soul becomes the only source of unity, and other
entities, therefore, lack a true unity of their own,
i.e., they lack a soul.

If God is equated with the principle of creativity
he is certainly Creator in a more dramatic sense than
Whiteheadian thought would allow. And so long as one
ignores the implications of the term absolute in this
formulation, it appears to be another step in reconciling Process to more traditional theologies. Once
the implications of the term absolute are introduced,
the formulation becomes contradictory.

We have used Thronton, Pittenger, Meland and
Cobb to illustrate a group of Whiteheadian influenced
Process theologians who make various efforts to get
around the Whiteheadian distinction between God and
creativity. Their attempts arise from a desire to
avoid the Process implications that come from making
God's absolute pole less than the unity of all reality.

225

1 Meland, Bernard Eugene. THE REALITIES OF FAITH.
    (New York: Oxford, 1962). p. 46.
2 ibid. p. 49.   3 p. 94   4 p. 163
5 p. 164.   6 p. 207.   7 pp. 258-259.
8 Cobb. A CHRISTIAN NATURAL THEOLOGY. p. 243.
9 ibid. p. 188.   10 p. 48.   11 p. 189.
12 p. 191   13 p. 206.   14 p. 211.

CHAPTER XXIV

WHITEHEADIANS, TEILHARDIANS
AND THEOLOGIANS OF HOPE

In earlier Chapters attention was given to the
works of Teilhard de Chardin. This was done for two
reasons. First of all Teilhard's thinking was a product of many of the same influences which contributed
to other Process philosophies. His writings, though
not generally available before the 1950's, fit into
our period of study. Second, his formulations were
very helpful in setting out the Process position.

From what has already been said about Teilhard, it
is clear that he could well be seen as an influence on
theology. A new awareness of Whitehead and the wide
response to the publication of Teilhard's works have
developed alongside one another, with little thought of
the combined influence of these two men on theology.
One notable exception to this fact was the 1973,
publication of HOPE AND THE FUTURE OF MAN by the London
Teilhardian society.1 It is a collection of papers
from a conference among Whiteheadians, Teilhardians,
and Theologians of Hope held at Union Theological
Seminary in New York City. As the title of the book
suggests, the chief topic of the conference was that
of eschatology. In spite of the limited scope of this
work, it serves as an introduction to the probable
development of a third trend in modern Process theology.

John Cobb, one of the conference participants, in
speaking of Whitehead, says that while his Process
view has a clear element of anticipation for the
future, Whitehead places the locus of value in the
present. While Cobb understands that others have a
specific future in mind, he says,

But Whitehead did not share that
vision. For him, the course of
events has neither beginning nor
end.2

On the other hand, as Philip Hefner points out, the future for Teilhard is more specific.

> To sum up, it is impossible to
> understand the future except
> relative to a deep probing of the
> past-present of which it _is_ the
> future. It is impossible to under-
> stand the past-present (which is the
> present identity of man and the
> world) except relative to the
> future which reveals what it is
> destined to become.3

Here is the key issue. Teilhard sees the present as influencing a rather specific future. Whitehead sees the present as contributing to an infinite process of becoming. This difference in outlook explains the basis for two somewhat different theological developments.

Another point which we made was that the distinction between God's absolute pole and creativity had a great influence upon all Whiteheadian based formulations. Wolfhart Pannenberg points to this very issue as being another source of the division between the Teilhardians and Whiteheadians:

> To be sure also in Whitehead's
> perspective God is the source of
> unity providing the subjective aim
> for every occasion which realizes
> itself by a process of subjective
> unification of its world. Could
> not this unifying activity be
> interpreted to mean a degree of
> participation in God's act of
> creation in the sense of Teilhard's
> creative unification? The difficulty
> is that creativity in Whitehead's
> own thought is separated from his
> idea of God.4

Daniel Day Williams in his response to Pannenberg clarifies the point that Whiteheadians do not totally split creativity off from God. We did also demonstrated this by referring to God as the objectification of creativity. Of course, it is true that God and creativity are not to be equated. As Williams says, "What Whiteheadians do say is that the unity of the creative process is to be found in the community of God's being with his creatures, not in the absolute unity which is summed up in a final event."5

The German school of theology called The Theology of Hope, in which Jurgen Moltmann, Wolfhart Pannenberg and Johannes Metz are included, is a third modern theological tradition with interesting parallels, and differences, to Whiteheadian thought. The views on eschatology is an example of an area in which Williams sees Theologians of Hope at issue with Whiteheadians.

> Now what does Professor Pannenberg see
> in process thought which differs from
> his position? This, I think: he sees
> process theology as having a more
> loosely organized universe in which
> there is an endless plurality of
> events; and therefore no final event
> which consummates or determines the
> unity of the whole.6

In view of the above illustrations, it becomes clear that creativity and absoluteness are some of the issues which can sharply divide thinkers inside and outside of the Whiteheadian tradition. Of course, we have not fully presented either Theology of Hope nor Teilhardian theology. We have merely suggested, in very general terms, some of the ways in which Whiteheadian influence on theology opens discussions with other important braches of contemporary thought. Moreover, our discussions of process theology have not included all of its contributors. What we have tried to do is include the chief trends in process theology as they developed following the developments in Process thought made by Whitehead.

1 HOPE AND THE FUTURE OF MAN. ed., Evert H. Cousins.
    (3 Cromwell Place, London: The Teilhardian
    Center For The Future Of Man, 1973).
2 Cobb, John B.,Jr. "What Is The Future? A Process
    Perspective." ibid. pp.5-7.
3 Hefner, Philip. "The Future As Our Future. A
    Teilhardian Perspective." ibid. p. 17.
4 Pannenberg, Wolfhart. "Future And Unity". ibid. p.64.
5 Williams, Daniel Day. "Response To Wolfhart
    Pannenberg." ibid. pp. 86-87.
6 Williams. p. 85.

CHAPTER XXV

CONCLUSIONS

What is Process Philosophy? Clearly this question can be answered in several different ways. One could say that it is a philosophy which takes the human experience of change seriously -- ultimately seriously. Another definition might be that Process is a philosophical response to the biological theory of evolution and the physical theory of relativity. Both of these explanations have certain merits, and could not be called wrong. However, Plato and Hegel, who are not called Process philosophers, certainly concerned themselves with the significance of change. The emphasis on change is not quite adequate as the way of fitting Process into the history of philosophy.

Likewise, evolution and relativity influenced the rise of philosophies other than Process, including neo-vitalism and neo-mechanism. Furthermore, while Process styled many of its formulations in response to positions taken by various natural sciences, other of the Process formulations pre-date modern science to the time of Plato and Aristotle; and are better understood as responses to differing philosophies. Responsiveness to the theories of evolution and relativity does not capture the total significance of Process.

However, it is impossible to appreciate what modern Process is attempting to suggest philosophically without a careful reference to certain important scientific developments of the late nineteenth and early twentieth centuries. To reach an adequate understanding of Process, one must analyze it in such a way that it is seen simultaneously in the context of the histories of science and philosophy. This work has been an effort to discuss Process thought, while keeping in mind the above demands.

In the early Chapters we saw the issues that developed in science when the physical theory of mechanism began to come into conflict with the modern

sciences of biology and psychology. Mechanism assured
continuity and causality by asserting that physical
laws were absolute. Neo-vitalism insisted upon the
necessity of true individuality and freedom, which
meant ultimate pluralism and the relativity of laws.
Mechanistic formulations demanded an 'absolute' when
they suggested that unity cannot be accounted for without changeless laws. Vitalistic formulations argued
that the absolute laws are predetermining, and must
therefore be rejected as eliminating the possibility of
plurality. However, vitalism was left with the problem
of accounting for unity.

Process thinkers observed that for themselves the
real significance of vitalism was that it experimentally demonstrated that the activity of life,
especially self-conscious life, required both unity and
diversity. As the concept of absolute physical laws
seemed to eliminate true diversity in the material
world, the source of activity could not be innate to
matter. Mechanism had merely taken the fact of the
activity for granted, without stopping to consider that
when the term absolute, which usually suggests ultimate
unity, is applied to a principle that governs the
activity of all reality, the diversity required for
activity cannot be explained.

Vitalism appeared to be justified in suggesting
that some 'vital force' had to be the real source of
activity. However, the vital force could not be
totally random activity. Even the activity of life
appeared to follow certain organizations. Of course,
if the unity factor in the vital force had been
referred to as absolute, then vitalism would have had
the same problem as mechanism, regarding true
diversity.

What was required for vitalism was a cosmic
activity in which a principle of unity and a principle
of diversity were the relata. This point having been
accepted by Process, there remained the problem of
deciding what was the nature of the activity that
related these two factors. The most widely adopted
model for what relates unity and diversity was that of

232

an organism. Generally, the universe was thought of as a single conscious organism, which divided itself into parts, thereby allowing for internal relationships.

However, it appeared that, as the entire universe was unified by the cosmic organism, it was perfectly correct to refer to the organic principle as absolute. Whitehead observed that this formulation continued to imply that the universe was determined by the nature of the organic principle. In other words, the unity of any part of the cosmic organism was in fact the unity of the whole organism; and its parts, therefore, made no distinctive contributions to unity.

The only way to avoid determinism of the activity of entities in the universe, said Whitehead, was to think of each entity as being an organism in its own right. That is, every entity was to enjoy its own unique unity. Of course, to think of each entity as being 'absolute' would lead to ultimate pluralism. Therefore, Whitehead suggested that in the wider sense absoluteness should apply only to the unity of the actual entity God. Of course, in the narrow sense all entities have 'individual absoluteness'. To understand this conclusion we must look once more at the term absolute.

Whitehead noted that the term absolute had been used in two respects. In mechanism, and in some forms of vitalism, it had referred to an abstract principle of unity. On the other hand, philosophy used the term to refer to a concrete unity whose content was all of reality. Whitehead saw that both of these understandings made valid points. However, in formulating a consistent concept of absoluteness they needed to be combined in some fashion.

If unity was correctly thought of as an abstract principle, then mechanism afforded no solution as to why this unity was not presently realized. Likewise, if all reality was already concretely unified by the Absolute, as some philosophy suggested, there was no accounting for present activity. On the other hand, if the term absolute referred to both a concrete unity,

and also an abstract concept of unity, then he saw a
way that unity could exist along with diversity, and
activity could be explained. Whitehead argued that
the concrete unity of the universe was the past. The
past alone absolutely organized and determined. He
assigned the whole of the past to the concrete content
of the absolute pole of God. As the present became
actualized it moved into the unity of the past.
Therefore, the past was also an abstract principle of
Unity. Thus understood, the absolute pole allowed for
an indeterminate future.

No finite entity unifies the whole of the past.
Therefore, Whitehead assigned the term absolute to the
infinite entity God, who alone holds the whole of the
past in the present of his absolute pole. Explaining
why Whitehead referred to the divine unity as
absolute, does not explain the nature of that unity,
which assures diversity, and is shared by all entities.
In taking up the question of the unity of the present
we began to move more clearly into the field of
philosophy.

The place of Process within the history of philosophy was the second topic considered. The field of
philosophy during the late nineteenth and early
twentieth centuries was roughly divided between the
Positivists and Romanicists; the former being the
materialists and the latter the spiritualists. The
spiritualists, generally influenced by the Kantian
and Hegelian traditions, believed that their positions
could be held against positivists, as no supportable
alternative to idealistic epistemology could be presented. Idealistic formulations demanded an Absolute
Subject, who held in unity a plurality of changeless
forms. These forms served to organize or limit the
conscious activity of organisms. The idealistic
epistemology, if accepted, led directly to a metaphysical position -- determinism. In this regard the
positivists and the spiritualists were quite the same.
The former saw reality organized by material laws; the
latter understood that it was organized by forms --
and sometimes by a spiritual subject, God.

The argument for relativism, i.e., pluralism, entered the field of epistemology at this time with renewed force. The traditional opponents of the idealists had been the realists. Traditional realism had always suggested that knowledge -- at least in part -- was relative. It was relative to a given subject's perception of a given object. This, of course, implied a plurality of subjects and objects.

The great strength of idealism had been its ability to account for the unity of knowledge. Realism on the other hand, had as its strength to nicely explain the errors and differences of perceptions, but had trouble explaining the unity of consciousness.

Process saw that part of the problem facing idealistic epistemology was a confusion over the implications of the term absolute. In terms of conscious activity, idealism suggested that the term absolute referred to a unity which served for the evaluation of mental data, but clearly this unity did not totally determine mental activity. In other words, the limitation of conscious activity allowed for diversity. Metaphysically, on the other hand, the term absolute referred to an ultimate concrete unity which did not allow for diversity.

In giving the term absolute the same reference in both epistemology and metaphysics, Whitehead argued that every actual entity, including God, had its own unique past as a principle of limitation. As we have already said, to God's past Whitehead gave the title absolute pole. Furthermore, Whitehead said that what makes unique history possible is that all entities share in the principle of activity, called creativity.

Thus there are for Whitehead two forms of unity. The first is the absolute pole in God. The second is the common principle of creativity shared by all entities, including God. However, the principle of creativity is not called absolute. In the first place creativity has no concrete content; it is pure activity, yet to be made concrete. The only unity with any concrete content, in an ultimate sense, is God's

absolute pole. In the second place creativity does not
serve as a principle of limitation; it is sheer potential. Only the past, i.e., God's absolute pole, places
limits on the whole of the universe.

The above understanding not only allows for the
free activity of finite entities, but it actually
promotes it. If an entity confronted an infinity of
possibilities, it would be unable to act. By limiting
the number of possibilities, the past makes the future
possible. Whitehead speaks of God providing an initial
'aim' for all entities, when he wishes to make clearer
that the past allows for the future, i.e., that limitation makes activity possible.

By presenting an analysis of the developments in
Process thought, we have arrived at a way of defining
Process. We have defined Process as a trend in
twentieth century philosophy, and not as the discovery
of a single thinker. The chief problem has been to
discover the basis upon which the various strands of
Process' development could be related. Apart from
such a basis the conclusions of Process thinkers can
appear unclear.

For example, when one first encounters the term
absolute in Whitehead's writings, its meaning appears
to be foreign to a usual understanding. However, as
we have shown, this is not the case. The Process
understanding of absoluteness is reached only after a
thorough analysis of what the term implied for thinkers
in the sciences and philosophy. Of course, as we have
seen, the term absolute is also especially helpful in
illustrating how Process thought developed. Indeed,
the development of specific understandings of absoluteness and creativity is one of the very things that
distinguishes Process.

Just how the Process positions affected the field
of theology was the topic of our last Chapters. Here,
with particular reference to the Process positon held
by Whitehead, we gave further attention to the
principle of creativity. Knowledge of this principle

depended upon an object. The objectification of the
principle of creativity is God.

God was further described as an actual entity;
that is, as having an absolute and a relative pole.
The absolute pole represents the ultimate category of
the 'one', but as a concrete object it is the particular
unity of all realized possibilities of relatedness.
Therefore, God has absoluteness in the sense that his
is a unity of all relationships.

Here we attempted to show that the idea of absoluteness and creativity used by Process helped to shape
the reasoning behind some of the most important developments among Process theologians. We also made
special reference to the influence of these understandings upon Christology, soteriology and eschatology.
The details of this influence have been analyzed, and
do not need to be repeated.

What will be useful, however, is a summary of the
consequences of the Process understanding of the
absolute pole for the whole of its thought. Such a
procedure will allow us to better demonstrate the broad
character of Process.

To begin with, mankind, according to Process, is
a perishing event in an infinity of change. The
absolute pole is powerless to bring creation of new
relationships to a termination. Of course there is
harmony within the absolute pole; a unity cannot be
otherwise. However there is no possibility of the
cosmos ever being taken up into that pole. Cosmic
harmony, whatever that might mean, cannot include
changelessness. Furthermore, all our experiences lead
to the conclusion that change can produce error,
disharmony, destruction and suffering. The new which
is produced by change always includes the possibility
of disaster.

Men seem anxious about change, and no philosophy
appreciates this fact better than Process. God has been
a source of comfort from the fear of change; He who

was called changeless could be appealed to as the preserver alone. No, says Process, this simply is not the case. If God is changeless, then he has no concern for mankind. If he changes, we cannot turn to him as an escape from change. God for Process is powerless to comfort those who are afraid to perish as individuals, and who find no comfort in the fact that the whole of the past is preserved in God.

In our day, many find it quite satisfactory to get along while accepting the idea that, if God exist at all, he is powerless. Those of this group who are humanitarians sometimes look to the possibility of mankind -- human society -- forming at least a temporary utopia. Unfortunately, such utopias are often based upon the concept of conformity. Undoubtedly man can learn to conform. Clearly this will not stop the process in the cosmos.

Give escape from change or utopian concepts theological expressions, and we have one way of understanding the two great doctrines of salvation: Nirvana and Heaven as popular concepts. Process denies both. Nor, as should now be clear, can God change this situation. He cannot even send his son to create the possibility of a perfect harmony.

If Process is right, and man cannot escape change, then the alternative is for man to use change. The complaint is sometimes made that the modern world changes too fast. Perhaps it does not yet change fast enough. To be more specific, it seems that some areas of human activity, such as the social sciences, cannot keep pace with the natural sciences. Therefore, the argument is made that there is merit in stopping, or slowing, change.

Process would only object to this. If there is value at all, that value must be understood within change. It is the results of change, after all, that shape reality. This is where Process sees God as providing a certain kind of security. It is the security that no new efforts lack meaning; as they remain an everlasting aspect of reality.

Of course, some harmful changes might well bring results that most men would feel hardly comforted to know were everlasting. It is true that Process goes on to point out that even the worst changes, by creating a new unity, open new possibilities that otherwise would not have been available. Ultimately, Whitehead believes, God's goodness will assure that these possibilities will counteract the harm done.

This is quite logical. The absolute pole does have the power to make a unity out of all relationships. The results of this new unity may well be positive to some entities and harmful to others. The point seems to be, that while a man cannot be assured that his actions will bear good fruits for him, he may well be assured that what he does will be good for some entity at some time. As Process never ends, entities continue to exit because of whatever unity is the absolute pole. The absolute pole has the power to assure that nothing can be ultimately destructive to all entities - - this is how God's goodness must be understood.

On the other hand, the more possibilities that are opened to human action, the greater is the chance that some of those will provide the pssibilities that man himself requires. That is, the greater will man's chance be that he can adjust to change. Here is the key. Value is understood in terms of change, and value is enjoyed if one is able to adjust to change. As change is inevitable, man's hope is to assure that some of the possibilities opened up by change are of value to him. This is possible because participation in the very nature of change is open to man as it is to all entities. In other words, man's hope is his being the forerunner of change. The more he incorporates change, the more he becomes like God.

Teilhard, for example, suggested that man could adjust to change through an increasing emphasis upon research. That is, he could acquire the knowledge to participate in change consciously, by understanding

and directing it. Here God's absolute pole is a real
help. As we have said before, it assures that changes
will occur and count. They cannot be meaningless.

Of course, there is no justification to the
suggestion that Process promotes research only within
the natural sciences. Indeed, the concept may apply to
research in any field, including theology. No one
could, for example, deny that Jesus, Buddha, and
Muhammed opened countless possibilities for mankind.
Unfortunately, religions tend to see their accomplish-
ments in terms of final and static achievements, rather
than as possibilities to be taken up and developed.

Clearly Process cannot be viewed as consistent
with dogmatic formulations of religion. Dogmas may
provide insights into new possibilities of knowledge,
but the dogmas themselves must be developed rather than
advocated. They are akin to scientific hypotheses
which remain useful for a period of time, but fade more
and more into the background as new experiences are
uncovered. For example, the Christian Process
theologian is one who attempts to develop all of the
possibilities that a particular dogma might offer.
This means that dogmas must necessarily receive
greatly diverse interpretations. Important dogmas are
those which allow many developments. Any dogma may
finally be exhausted, but its worth will have been
judged by how far it has carried man into new possibilities.

Religious communities should best be understood
as groups of people involved in the research and
development of dogmas. Their conhesiveness will not
be based on agreement, but on the mutual benefit
acquired through their enjoyment of new possibilities.
Furthermore, there is no reason to assume that dogmas,
from which they work, must be borrowed from a
single tradition.

The careful study of Process leads us to conclude
that many of its implications come into conflict with
traditional Christian theological formulations. But

240

this need not remain a permanent dilemma.

Not only is Process useful because of its conclusions, but it also interesting because of the
methodology that it follows. Therefore, we will
end with a summary of the Process methodology.

Speaking of everything from ethics to perceptions
as 'relative' is far more consistent with common usage
that many persons realize. However, in the popular
understanding of relativity there is a danger of its
becoming a modern hedonism. In both the individual
serves as the point of reference for decision to act.
The difference being that in the former, ulike in the
latter, the individual depends upon the objective
reality of his relationships. Relationships may be
engaged in purely for one's advantage. Man's waste-
fulness of natural resources is just such a relationship. The general argument put forward to discourage
a hedonistic way of viewing the individual as 'the'
point of reference is that if one does those things
which reduce the possibilities of his continuing to
have relationships, he is engaged in self-injury.
Continuing with our above illustration: if man wastes
his natural resources, the human species will die out
for want of food, fuel and water. This we might call
the commonsense check on the dangers of the popular
understanding of relativity.

Thus we suggest that the idea that an individual
depends upon relationships is not an uncommon understanding. This means that the consideration of the
implications of relationships becomes a valuable source
of information for a decision to act. The problem for
commonsense is setting the 'limits' on any attempt to
analyze the relationships that must be considered,
respective to a decision to act; because in a relative
universe, says Process, relationships in the abstract
are infinite.

We may finally move directly to our point that
Process has a methodology. In particular it is a way
of dealing with the modern theory of relativity. Its

usefulness can be understood as a way of understanding what the term absolute refers to in a relative universe. It provides a special understanding of 'fact': a single fact is a limitation, rather than an 'absolute'. It is a limitation resulting from the particular relationships constituting the perspective of a given individual or group of individuals. The term absolute refers to the totality of realized relationships, of which single facts are a part of the concrete content.

The role of the Process philosopher can be to guide men in selecting the most appropriate limits; that is, to help men draw the line at how many relationships must be taken into consideration, realizing that total knowledge of concrete relatedness is available only to God, before a decision to act can be reached. Furthermore, as the facts upon which any decision is made are now understood as a part of relatedness, no decision to act can excuse men from continuing to do research into the whole of relatedness. No topic can ever be closed from further investigation. This is what Teilhard implied when he spoke of more and more human energy going into research.

If the above paragraph sounds rather like a scientist's view of truth, our point is being well made. Many of the greatest Process thinkers, Whitehead and Teilhard included, were men of science. While one must deplore the inadequate background in the natural sciences given to many students, Process methodology is not useless to those disciplines far removed from the natural sciences. Indeed, a scientist, who is in fact a technician, would find Process methodology as foreign to him as would the theologian who functions as a dogmatist.

The comparison just made will be clearer as we outline and develop the Process methodology. It may be summarized as being composed of three major elements. First it assumes that facts are concrete limitations of reality. They are useful but not definitive, and they depend upon God as a principle of limitation. Second it assumes that the more relationships considered within a decision to act, the more valuable will be the results, with the following qualification: The role of the expert, including the theologian and the scientist, is to determine the narrow margin between sufficient consideration of relationships and a confusion of data. Such expertise is achieved by research. However, research does not mean the elimination of commonsense. Third, the results of actions are assumed to elude absolute prediction, even by God. Therefore, the methodology assumes originality. Limitation, research, and originality: these are the three key insights into the adoption of a Process methodology.

Limitation for Process is based upon three principles: heredity, chance and God. With the fairly recent discovery of DNA and RNA, genetic research has achieved a new level of understanding. Whatever one might have believed in the past, modern genetic research must surely influence all thinking about the place of man in the universe. Of course, the details of such research must be left in the hands of those trained in the relevant disciplines. However, the trend of their discoveries is quite consistent with a Process understanding of the past as a principle of limitation. Man's particular genetic development, covering perhaps billions of years, imposes the great limitation that a fairly narrow range of conditions are necessary for the survival of his species.

Moving to the factor of chance, as an aspect of limitation, we enter into a rather difficult topic. Students of heredity, since Darwin, have talked about chance as an element in the evolutionary process of adaptation. On the other hand, most Process thinkers introduce chance as a factor in discussions of mathematical or logical 'probability'. An adequate comparison of what chance means in these various disciplines has never been made. However, there does seem to be consistent agreement on the point that chance should not too quickly be associated with freedom or indeterminism. Rather, chance is more correctly included within a discussion of limitation.

For example, a given individual's chance development of certain of his genetic characteristic or potentials -- often at the cost of others -- gives him a decided advantage in particular situations. Therefore, one might explain biological chance as the skills which a given individual has developed, respective to this situation in which he is forced to function.

Many will soon see that heredity and chance help to make up what we have called limitation. However, when God is introduced the meaning may be obscure. Therefore, we might be reminded that one of God's functions is to present a universal spectrum for chance; somewhat similar to that spectrum introduced for the individual by his heredity.

Because we live in a universe of relativity, i.e., all things are related, every human action necessarily has universal significance. Yet the problem for commonsense is to place the concept of 'universal significance' of human actions into a meaningful perspective. In Cobb's opinion, as we saw, the greatness of a religion rests in its ability to allow its adherents to discover such meaningfulness. Norman Pittenger and Teilhard de Chardin, agreeing, with Cobb, judge Christianity very highly because its doctrine of love supplies a meaningful perspective in which all actions can be universally related. Thus to show love in a particular relationship is to act in univerally valid fashion.

One of the ways in which Process supports the Christian idea of 'love' relationships is its contention that God's concrete nature is a unity of relationships. Relationships, i.e., actions which promote unity, are of greatest value to the cosmos. Only in the formation of unities are there new possibilities opened for entities.

A fact is a limitation based on a reference to heredity, chance and God. Fact is relative both to the individual and to the whole universe. Having now discussed the basis of fact, we must move to the 'establishment' of fact by research. Of course, research can be carried out in every field, but, because of the Process understanding of limitation, the three most critical areas of research are biology-genetics, physics-logic (including mathematics as their expression), and philosophy-theology.

One of the more perplexing tasks for modern thought has been attempts at classification of the sciences. We are not attempting any such classification. Nevertheless, it seems clear that even a brief survey of Process thinkers will reveal the emphasis placed upon the three areas of research mentioned above.

Finally we come to the concept of originality. Research at its best will allow the greatest number of relationships to be clearly considered in terms of a decision to act. Yet the very nature of limitation and research allows for a field of 'indetermination' which demands an original approach.

Unfortunately an understanding of 'indeterminate' is usually reached through a concept such as the 'unknown future.' However, the future is not something to be discovered. It is something to be created, according to the Process understanding. We must keep a clear distinction between the concepts of the future and of an indeterminate field of actions. One may say anything about the future or nothing. The two are one in the same. As the future is an infinity of possibilities, anything might be correct.

What is commonly called the present is the real indeterminate field. It is the field of action qua action. Whenever an action takes place new relations are set up with consequences that even the most thorough research could not have predicted. In this sense action is discontinuous with the past. Of course, in many cases the discontinuity cannot be observed. However, in the wider sense we do experience discontinuity as growth, development, movement -- the

dynamic aspect of reality. At this point the reader
may draw back in disbelief. Surely there is nothing
which demonstrates continuity better than the growth
of a fetus.

If this is true, then diversity and movement cannot be explained. If all movement is absolute
continuity, then human action has no ulitmate meaning.
An absolute continuity implies that action is predetermined. A predetermined action has no value of
itself. Process thought firmly insists upon the
ultimate meaningfulness of action, which demands a
corresponding field of indeterminateness. However, as
we have tried to make clear, this field cannot be one
of infinite possibility. Such a field would in itself
make action impossible. Therefore, within a given
present there must be a finite number of possibilities,
i.e., of possible relationships. This finite number
is indeterminate in two ways. First, it can be
indeterminate in the sense that only a certain number
of the possible relationships will be realized. Second
it is always indeterminate in the exact results of the
relationships that are realized. This means that
Process must hold that no relationship is always true
in terms of giving specific results. Originality is
needed in order to deal creatively with this situation.

None of the above observations about Process
thinking would deny the point that God, because of his
unique perspective, 'knows' the possible future with
the highest degree of probability. Indeed, it would
seem that the theological concepts of God's
omniscience and human freedom might be finally reconciled by modern theories of probability.

It may well serve as a review of what we have
been saying if we examine how the present comes to be
an indeterminate field, as opposed to an infinity of
possibilities. In other words, we need to explain why
the fact of discontinuity does not deny the present
unity of reality. The obvious answer is that some
ultimate continuum or principle of unity must have a
place in reality.

Whitehead, we may remember, calls this ultimate
principle creativity. Another way of speaking of the
continuum between the whole of the past and the whole
of the present is that the continuity results from
relativity itself. The universe is always the same --
relative. To speak of a relative universe, in the
Whiteheadian sense, is to speak of entities unified by
a present potential for relatedness. This insight
becomes the ultimate basis which Process offers for
a commonsense understanding of relativity. Man is not
determined by his being related to other entities in
the universe, rather man is the indeterminate potential
to relate to all other entities. In his relations,
therefore, man helps to determine the universe rather
than only being determined by it.

If theologians find the Process methodology
foreign to their immediate assumptions, that is
understandable. In general, however, Process as a
philosophy need not be closely associated with
theology. It may be a useful tool for theology;
as it is for other disciplines. However, no field
exhausts the usefulness of Process. In some ways
contemporary Process thought is beginning to once
again move out of the field of theology. The return
of Process thinkers to the mainstream of philosophy
and natural science is a Chapter in its development
that is yet to be written.

ADDITIONAL BIBLIOGRAPHY

Berdyaev, Nicolas. THE DESTINY OF MAN. trans., Natalie Duddington. (London: Centenary Press, 1937).

Bergson, Henri. MIND-ENERGY. trans., H. Wildon Carr. (London: Macmillan, 1920).

Brightman, Edgar Sheffield. THE PROBELEM OF GOD. (New York: Abingdon, 1930).

PROCESS PHILOSOPHY AND CHRISTIAN THOUGHT. eds., Delwin Brown, Ralph E. James, Jr., and Gene Reeves. (New York: Bobbs-Merrill, 1971).

Cobb, John B., Jr. LIBERAL CHRISTIANITY AT THE CROSSROADS. (Philadelphia: Westminster, 1973).

Comte, Auguste. THE CATECHISM OF POSITIVE RELIGION. trans., Richard Congreve. (London: Kegan Paul, 1891).

Edington, A.S. THE NATURE OF THE PHYSICAL WORLD. (Cambridge: University Press, 1928).

Einstein, Albert. RELATIVITY THE SPECIAL AND THE GENERAL THEORY. trans., Robert Lawson. (London: Methuen, 1921).

..... SIDELIGHTS ON RELATIVITY. trans., G.B. Jeffery & W. Perrett. (London: Methuen, 1922).

..... THE MEANING OF RELATIVITY. trans., Edwin Adams. (London: Methuen, 1922).

Findlay, J.N. ASCENT TO THE ABSOLUTE. (London: George Allen & Unwin, 1970).

Hartshorne, Charles. THE PHILOSOPHY AND PSYCHOLOGY OF SENSATION. (Chicago University Press, 1934).

PHILOSOPHERS SPEAK OF GOD. ed., Charles Hartshorne, and William Reese. (Chicago University Press, 1953).

..... "What Did Anselm Discover?" THE MANY FACED ARGUMENT. eds., John Hick and Arthur McGill. (London: Macmillan, 1968).

PROCESS AND DIVINITY. "The Hartshorne Festschrift." eds., William L. Reese and Eugene Freeman. (LaSalle: Open Court, 1964).

Hicks, G. Daws. CRITICAL REALISM. (London: Macmillan, 1938).

Hocking, William Ernest. HUMAN NATURE AND ITS REMAKING. (Yale University Press, 1918).

THE NEW REALISM. eds., Edwin B. Holt, Walter T. Marvin,

et. al. (New York: Macmillan,1912).

James, William. A PLURALISTIC UNIVERSE. (London: Longmans, Green, 1909).

..... SOME PROBLEMS OF PHILOSOPHY. (London: Longmans, Green, 1911).

Lossky, N.O. THE WORLD AS AN ORGANIC WHOLE. trans., Natalie A. Duddington. (Oxford University Press, 1928).

Lowe, Victor. UNDERSTANDING WHITEHEAD. (Johns Hopkins University Press, 1962).

RELIGIOUS REALISM. ed., D.C. MacIntosh (New York: Macmillan, 1931).

Montague, William P. THE WAYS OF THINGS. (New York: Prentice-Hall, 1940).

Northrop, F.S.C. THE MEETING OF EAST AND WEST. (New York: Collur Books, 1966).

Sherburne, Donald W. A WHITEHEADIAN AESTHETIC. (Yale University Press, 1961).

Simpson, G. Gaylord. THE MEANING OF EVOLUTION. (Yale University Press, 1952).

Thomson, J. Arthur. "The Influence Of Darwinism On Thought and Life." SCIENCE AND CIVILIZATION. ed., F.S. Marvin. (Oxford University Press, 1923). pp. 203-220.

Thornton, Lionel S. THE COMMON LIFE IN THE BODY OF CHRIST. (Westminster: Dacre Press, 1941).

Trethowan, Illtyd. THE ABSOLUTE AND THE ATONEMENT. (London: George Allen & Unwin, 1971).

Weiss, Paul. REALITY. (Princeton University Press, 1938).

..... MODES OF BEING. (Carbondale, Illinois: Southern Illinois University Press, 1958).

Whitehead, Alfred North. "The First Physical Synthesis". SCEINCE AND CIVILIZATION. ed., F.S. Marvin. (Oxford University Press, 1923). pp. 161-178.

Wieman, Henry Nelson. THE WRESTLE OF RELIGION WITH TRUTH. (New York: Macmillan, 1927).